FOR KAREN
Thanks for your love and patience
through all kinds of weather

Rock n' Blues Harmonica

Harp Knowledge, Songs, Stories, Lessons,
Riffs, Techniques
and Audio Index
For A New
Generation
of Harp Players

By
Jon Gindick

With illustrations by
Mark Zingarelli

Cross Harp Press
Visalia — Los Angeles

Introduction

The lights are low as you step onto the stage. In the audience, you see faces, the faces of people who have come to hear the hottest band in town–with you on blues harp.

The lights brighten and dim. This means it's time to start. "One-two-three-four," shouts the drummer. He bangs his sticks on the drumheads. The guitarist strums his opening chord, and the bass player dances across the stage, the boom of his instrument providing a low-toned support.

The music has started: a churning brew of of rhythm and sound that makes people move to their feet and out to the dance floor. Now it's your turn. You place the hand-cupped microphone and harp to your lips and, as naturally as speaking, begin drawing, blowing, bending, tongue-blocking the language of the blues.

There's a stir in the audience. Wow. This is the sound they've come to hear, and once again, you are glad you are a harp player. It's the sound of your harp supporting and leading the guitar, drums and bass. It's the sound of emotion and skill, creativity and fun. It's the sound of rock and blues harmonica. And, man, there's nothing else like it.

Rock n' Blues Harmonica is about this sound, this music, this attitude– and how a total beginner can turn him or herself into a blues harmonica musician. In Chapter I, you'll learn some basic concepts of blues music theory. In Chapter II, your great harmonica lesson begins–information mixed with jokes, stories, songs, riffs and exercises that let the skills and ideas of blues harp flow naturally to and from that subconscious boiler room in which creativity and music originate.

> This book is intended to be read harp in hand and mouth. To play with the CD, you need a ten-hole "C" diatonic harmonica.

An essential part of this program is the 74-minute CD that accompanies this book. Every beginning through intermediate harmonica technique is played and explained over a slow, continuous blues band "loop" that drives the reality of chord changes, and the anticipating of them, into your head.

It is my belief that, more than any other instrument, blues harmonica is a language unto itself. How do you learn a language? By immersing yourself in it: hearing it, speaking it, *living* it.

I invite you. Immerse yourself in the blues harmonica. Play with this CD, play solo, listen to other harp players, check out the local blues bands, buy some blues CDs, meet other harp players and learn from them. Most important, whether you're a real rocker or a wanna-be, playing *every* day makes success inevitable.

Things take time—including the learning of a language, or the playing of an instrument. You *can* play instant harmonica, and that is how it will sound: instant harmonica. Quick, painless, easy harping is how everyone starts. Have fun. Once you have that part down, create a five year learning program that lets you get better, and better, and better.

In this book:
uncircled numbers mean blow that hole
circled numbers mean draw
a dot means to tongue (or otherwise articulate)
* means bend half step
** means bend whole step
*** means bend a step and a half

Table of Contents

Here are the first six weeks of Music Theory 101 rolled into a 10-minute read. Music is built from notes, scales, harmonizing notes, chords and chord progressions. It will be helpful to have a basic understanding of how it all fits together. This beginner's story brings theory to life.

Start off like a cave man—just put the harp in your mouth and draw. Keep reading and playing, and you'll be playing chords, single notes, and octaves with sweet vibrato and precision articulation.

Now learn the ideas behind 2nd position, how and why it works, and where the Wailing Notes, Notes of Resolution and Stepping Stone Notes are located. The trick is to accent the draw notes, and play your **C** harp in the key of **G**.

Let's bring in the band and see how simple blues harp fits in even when you don't know what the heck you're doing.

A riff is a unit of music you use to build, sustain, change and resolve musical tension. Take a lesson around the harp from the Stone Age's best harp player, and get some good blues riffs into your heart.

Music is a wheel, and the spokes are chord progressions. Chapter VI shows where these notes are located on the harp and helps you use them to turn blues riffs into blues songs.

VII. Falling In Love With Bending

If you curve the drawn air down just right in the harmonica's air chamber, the pitch of the note will lower. Learning to bend can add 12 additional notes and let you speak, slur and slide your way into the blues. This chapter is for beginners and intermediates, and includes use of hands for compression and that talking sound.

VIII. Straight Harp Accompaniment

The Cave Boys get a chick singer and learn the hard way that some situations call for soft, melodic accompaniment. This easy chapter helps show you how good it can sound.

IX. Cross Harp Campfire Melodies

In 2nd position, play some of the greatest songs ever sung. Guitar chords are included for your play-along pleasure. Included is a special chart on transposing 1st position notation to 2nd position. Learning these songs in the blues style teaches you melody, bends and improvisations.

X. Third Position Slant Harp–A Big Time Harp Style

Now play your **C** harp in the key of **D** minor. It's easy and sounds great.

XI. Hubie's Blues–Intermediate and Advanced Harp or Everything I Almost Forgot to Put in the Book

This is advanced stuff on many issues: tuning your harp, mastering amplified harp, playing chromatic blues, tongue-blocking, playing harp in positions 1 through 6 plus 12.

Resource Guide and Record Index

Here's the key of harmonica you need to jam with classic harmonica recordings plus a listing of essential harmonica resources and Jon's other harmonica products.

ONE

The Night Music was Discovered

(Theory for Beginners)

It was a magical night. The stars were twinkling and everything was new – including music. This was the night Adam and Eve discovered the note, the chord, and the chord progression. It was the night music was born.

Eight Little Sounds

As everyone knows, music was discovered by Adam and Eve in the Garden of Rockin'.

Here's how it happened.

One morning, Adam was thirsty. He'd been running around the Garden discovering things and giving them names. He was hot and sweaty, so he asked Eve to bring him a glass of iced tea.

Now, Eve was a flaxen-haired beauty with great legs and a terrific sense of humor. She was also very intelligent. She filled a glass with tea and ice and handed it to Adam. As he took it from her hand, the spoon accidentally struck the glass.

What happened next was incredible. It was a sound, a high-pitched ringing tone. Eve's sensitive eardrums could feel this noise vibrating.

"What's that?" Eve asked.

Adam, of course, knew everything. And what he didn't know, he named. Still, he had no idea what that sound was.

"A..." he began.

"A what?" demanded Eve.

"A...a...it's an **A**," he said, and drank a little more of the tasty tea. As if by miracle, the spoon struck the glass once again.

The glass, being emptier by one swallow, made a tone that was one swallow higher.

"And what's that?" Eve asked.

"Do I have to tell you everything?" snapped Adam. "It's a **B**!" He gave Eve a smarter-than-thou look and sipped again from the glass.

"Typical male," Eve said. But the lady was getting curious. She tapped on the glass with the spoon. Being a little emptier than before, the resulting tone was a little higher.

"And I suppose that's a **C**," Eve said.

"You got it," muttered Adam. He took another swallow. "Tingggg!" sang the glass as Eve struck it with the spoon.

"For crimany sakes, woman," Adam growled. But they both knew that what had occurred was a **D**.

And so it went. Adam drank. Eve played an **E**. Adam sipped once more. Eve clanged a one-beat boogie on an **F**. Again Adam sipped. The new tone was dubbed **G**.

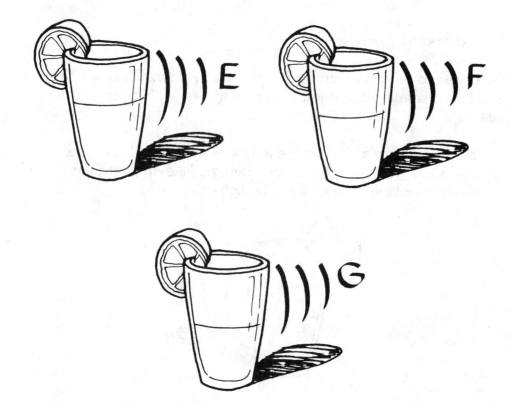

"Big deal," Adam said. He took another swallow. He had now drunk half the iced tea that was originally in the glass. Eve struck the glass with the spoon.

A sound occurred.

"Boy, that sounds familiar," said Eve.

"Of course,"Adam said. "It's the same note we played in the beginning." The highly caffeinated iced tea was beginning to have an effect on him.

"It's an **A**, but a higher **A** than we played when the glass was full. What we've done is play a ladder of sounds starting from **A**." And in his rich tenor voice Adam started to sing:

"**A B C D E F G A**!"

"You see, Eve, when the glass was full, and the spoon hit it, vibrations came out of the glass into the air. You may not believe this, but I counted 440 vibrations per second. That was the **A** sound.

"Now, I drank a little bit more and you banged the glass again. Since the glass was a bit emptier, the vibration into the air (and our eardrums) was faster. In fact, it was right around 510 vibrations per second. That's the sound we called a **B**."

"I get it," Eve said. "Each time you made the glass a little emptier, the vibrations it made were a little faster, and the resulting tone was higher. But why is the high **A** the same as the low **A**?"

"Don't you see?" Adam said. "The glass vibrated twice as fast, and that makes the sound twice as high."

"I suppose you think that makes you twice as smart," Eve said with a giggle.

"Of course," laughed Adam. "Now let's assign some names to all this. We'll call each sound a NOTE. That gives us an **A** note, a **B** note, a **C** note, and so forth.

"And each ladder of sounds that goes from **A** to **A**, or from **B** to **B** is a SCALE. If you start on an **A**, you have an **A** scale. If you start on a **C**, it's a **C** scale. Not bad, eh?"

"How come you have to name everything?" Eve asked. "Some strange psychological compulsion?"

"And the distance between a high **A** and the low **A**...we'll call that an OCTAVE."

"Call it what you want," Eve said. "Just answer me this. What's it good for?"

"Get me eight glasses of iced tea and we'll find out," Adam said.

Sweet Harmony

That evening, strange sounds were heard in the Garden. There was laughter. Then came a new way of talking that rose and fell in the craziest ways. And then, even weirder, came a succession of high-pitched, ringing sounds. *Bong! Clang! Boing!*

It was Adam and Eve, sitting in the glow of the fire, pleasantly blasted on bongo juice, surrounded by glasses, each filled with a different amount of iced tea. Adam was beating his hands on his haunches and snapping his fingers, giving Eve a rhythm in which to explore the tones of the glasses.

"Yeah, yeah," Adam sang. "Yeah, yeah."

"Hey!" cried Eve. "Listen to this!" She was holding a spoon in each hand. "If I strike a **C** note at the same time that I strike an **E**, dig it: the sounds combine."

Firelight flickering on her face, Eve clanged the spoons on the glass filled to **C** and on the glass filled to **E** at the same time.

The two tones collaborated and faded into the night.

"That was beautiful," Adam said. "Do it again."

Once again, Eve struck the **C** and **E** glasses at the same time. The vibrations intertwined to form something rich and sweet.

"What *was* that?" asked a delighted Eve.

"Think I'll call that a...a...a HARMONY," said Adam. "Yes, a harmony is when two notes played at the same time blend together to form a new, combined sound."

"Fair enough," said Eve. "But what happens if I strike the **C** and **D** glasses at the same time?"

To answer her own question, Eve banged her spoons on the two glasses.

Although the **C** and **D** did not clash, neither did they form the beautiful blend that came from the **C** and **E**. Eve frowned. What was going on here?

"I get it!" she suddenly cried. "The **C** and **E** notes are the first and third notes of the **C** scale. **C** is number 1, **D** is number 2, **E** is number 3, and so on.

"If you want a nice blending harmony using the **C**, you strike the 1st and 3rd notes of the **C** scale at the same time.

"And if you want this blend to use the **G** sound, you strike the 1st and 3rd notes of the **G** scale."

To prove her point, Eve struck her spoons on the **G** and **B** glasses. The two sounds combined beautifully.

18

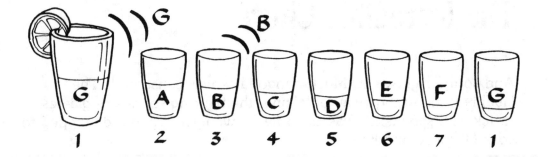

"See?" cried Eve. "If I play the 1st and 3rd notes of this simple scale at the same time, they merge together. I've got an idea. Let's call the 1st and 3rd notes HARMONIZING NOTES!"

Suddenly, Eve realized her mistake. It was Adam's job to name things. She could discover, but *he* had to name. She looked at him nervously. Would he be angry?

Adam only smiled. Eve looked beautiful with firelight rippling across her long, flowing hair. "Yeah," Adam said, a crazy grin on his face. "The 1st and 3rd notes come together and harmonize when played at the same time. Just like us, baby."

The Incredible Chord

And so the night went. Much bongo juice was consumed. The laughing, the strange way of talking, the piercing sounds of glasses struck with spoons...it was all so new. Even The Landlord stopped to cock His head and listen.

Meanwhile, the couple in the Garden were making important discoveries about this thing called music. They learned that not only did the 1st and 3rd notes of each scale come together and harmonize when played at the same time – but that the 5th note of the scale also harmonized.

Adam called this combination of three harmonizing notes played at the same time a CHORD. To play a **C** chord, Eve would strike the glasses that produced a **C** note and an **E** note, the 1st and 3rd notes of the **C** scale. At exactly the same time, Adam would bang on the 5th note of the scale – the **G** note.

The **C, E,** and **G** notes flowed into each other and produced what Adam called a **C** chord.

Then, Eve struck the 1st, 3rd and 5th notes of the **G** scale. **G** was the 1st note, **B** was the 3rd note and **D** was the 5th note. This produced the **G** chord.

the G major chord

G 1   B 3   D 5

"Hey!" shouted Adam. "I think we're on to something!"

Without thinking about what he was doing, he picked up the 6th glass
of the **C** scale and started to drink. He had half a swallow in his mouth
when Eve squealed, "What are you doing?"

Coughing, half-choking, face red with embarrassment, Adam put the
glass back in its number 6 spot. "I thought it was bongo juice," he
started to say, but stopped himself.

"I know exactly what I'm doing," he said imperiously.

"And what exactly is that?" demanded Eve.

"I wanted to see what would happen if I made the 6th note a little
higher by making the glass a half-swallow emptier. Know what I mean?
Now the glass is halfway between the 6th and 7th notes of the of the
C scale. It's a 6 1/2 glass."

"Real sharp, flathead!" shouted Eve.

But Adam knew the best discoveries often occurred by mistake.
"Let's see what happens when *you* play the 1st, 3rd and 5th notes
of the **C** scale at the same time that *I* bang on the 6½ note."

"Whatever you say," answered Eve. She banged her spoons on the 1st,
3rd and 5th glass while Adam played his 6½ glass.

---

*In later days, the 6½ scale degree would become known as "the flatted 7th".

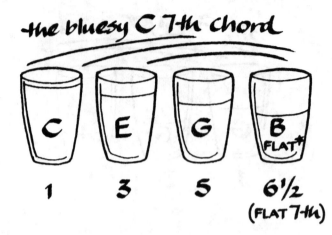

the bluesy C 7th chord

C   E   G   B FLAT*

1   3   5   6½ (FLAT 7th)

What a sound! It was odd, yet powerful, speaking of the ironies of a life filled with passions and disappointments, new loves and sad goodbyes. All this was pretty heady stuff for Adam who had spent all his young life in the Garden of Eden. Still, he must have had a sense of what was to come.

"This chord, this combination of 1st, 3rd, 5th and 6½ notes of a scale shall henceforth be called a 7th CHORD (in this case C7th)."

He looked triumphantly at Eve and wobbled a little. "And the 7th chord shall be the mainstay, the distinguishing characteristic of the type of music that will someday be called THE BLUES."

At that, Eve grabbed Adam and laughingly pulled him to the ground, covering him with kisses. "I'll give you the blues," she murmered, pulling him closer.

---

* The term **B** flat refers to the note halfway between the **A** and the **B**. This note could also be called **A** sharp, but rarely is. Including sharps and flats (also known as halfsteps), there are 12 notes in a scale: **A** flat, **A, B** flat, **B, C, C** sharp, **D, E** flat, **E, F, F**sharp, **G**.

Majors and Minors

Well, they played and played. All of it in the key of **C**, of course.

KEY? That's the word Adam used to identify the idea that in music, if you start a song on a **C** note, you usually end the song on a **C** note. Thus you're playing in the key of **C**.

In the same vein, when you start a song on an **E** note, you usually end the song on the **E** note – and are playing in the key of **E**.

At any rate, as Adam and Eve arranged and rearranged glasses and struck them with spoons, they learned a few things about music that would intrigue musicians for years to come.

1.   Woman likes to boogie as much as man.

2.   Clinking spoons on glasses of iced tea is a hell of a way to make music.

3.   When playing in the key of **C**, you can play the basic chord, the major chord, by striking the 1st, 3rd and 5th glasses of the scale.

4.   You can get a blues sound by including the $6\frac{1}{2}$ note with the 1st, 3rd and 5th.

5.   You can get a mysterious, eerie sounding chord by playing the 1st, $2\frac{1}{2}$ and 5th glasses of a scale. Adam called this a MINOR CHORD.

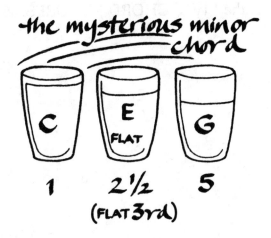

23

6. And, playing the 1st, 3rd, 5th and 6th produces a jazzy sounding chord. This was called a MAJOR 6th.

In fact, the list of chords Adam and Eve discovered that evening was endless. There were no limits on the tones these notes could combine to form.

As Eve went from one chord to the next, it was easy to imagine her the precursor of today's electric guitarist. She shook her head and her long hair swished back over her shoulder. She lifted her spoon-holding hands and brought them down in a wide arc, almost as though she were strumming the glasses.

"Yeah, yeah," Adam sang. Although he didn't know it, his girlfriend Eve was on the verge of a new discovery – a discovery that would create the chord framework for the types of music that would one day be known as country western, blues, punk, disco, reggae, folk, rock a' billy, gospel, tex-mex, schlock and rock and roll.

This discovery was the I-IV-V CHORD PROGRESSION. Here's how it happened.

The I-IV-V of Music

Eve arranged the iced-tea glasses into rows of major chords.

First, she bonged the **C** chord 4 times in a row. Then she clanged on the **F** chord, the chord 4 glasses up the scale from the **C**.

She played these two chords over and over and it sounded terrific. Four beats on the I chord, four beats on the IV chord. This was the birth of the TWO-CHORD JAM.

But there was much more to learn. This was when Eve discovered she could add to the two-chord feeling by bonging the **G** chord, the chord 5 glasses up the scale from the **C** chord.

This V chord (the **G** chord when played in the key of **C**) took the music further away from the I chord. It added a sense of transition, a feeling of drama and *tension*.

It sounded great to pound out a beat on the I chord, then the IV chord, then back to the I chord. Now was the time to play the V chord, slip down to the IV chord, and with an air of finality and resolution, return to the I chord.

Wow! This I-IV-V progression really made sense. It put the sounds into a cycle, gave them a beginning and an end. It created and resolved tension. It organized sound to tell a story.

Even Adam was amazed as Eve hunched over her rows of iced tea glasses and played these beautiful sequences of harmonizing notes. He *had* to jam. But how? How does one musician accompany another? Spoon in hand, the original man set out to make a new discovery.

Accompanying the I-IV-V Chord Progression

Adam knew Eve was playing her I-IV-V chord progression in the key of **C**. Following a hunch, he started banging on his **C** glass. It sounded pretty good! While Eve went from one chord to the next, all Adam had to do was play the 1st note of the scale.

But Eve, swinging spoons like a maestro, wanted more. "C'mon!" she shouted over the loud clinking of iced tea glasses. "Get it on!"

So get it on is exactly what Adam did. But he paid attention, too. Soon he realized that certain iced tea glasses sounded great no matter where the music was in the I-IV-V progression.

The glasses that always sounded so great were none other than the 1st, 3rd and 5th notes of the **C** scale. These were the harmonizing notes that made up the **C** chord.

By accenting these harmonizing notes (playing them longer and playing them louder), and using other notes in the **C** scale as stepping stones between one harmonizing note and another, Adam created melodic patterns that swirled confidently through Eve's I-IV-V progression of chords.

Amazingly, it didn't matter when Adam hit the 1st, 3rd or 5th note. Each would work at any point in the chord progression.

Now Adam decided to get fancy. He started banging on the 2½ glass, the glass which was left over from the minor chord. What a sound! Sexy, sultry, bluesy. He banged the 2½ glass again, and *again*. Like the 1st, 3rd and 5th notes, it worked through all of Eve's chord changes.

But this 2½ note did more than simply accompany the I-IV-V chord progression. Somehow, it changed the music, made it hard. Made it tense. Made it bluesy.

It was a BLUES HARMONIZING NOTE.

2½ (FLAT 3rd)

"Alright!" shouted Eve. As the original blues lady bonged a steady beat on the I-IV-V progression, Adam explored every nook and cranny of the **C** scale. He banged the 1st note six or seven times (it didn't matter). Then he clanged the 5th note, the 4th note, the 2½ note, and finally returned to the 1st note.

Then he was off again, at one time or another striking a spoon on every glass he could see. Some glasses sounded terrible, and some sounded like they were born to make music. Finally, through trial and error, Adam discovered the BLUES SCALE.

Starting with the **C** note and going up the scale, the blues scale went: 1 2½ 4 5 6½ 1.*

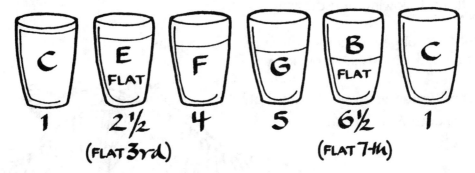

What a sound this blues scale created! What a feeling! Eve, by now, was playing progressive jazz chords, using minors, major sixths, altering the chord progression in innumerable ways, playing rock, reggae, blues and country western, yet never leaving the key of **C**. Adam, too, was swept away by the ringing tones of iced tea glasses. Eve could play any chord she wanted, and as long as she always returned to her **C** chord, her I chord, Adam's wonderful new blues scale would not make a mistake.

This was the kind of music that could go on forever. (And in a way, it has.) But even the original man and woman occasionally got tired.

As the sun rose in the eastern sky and the light of a new day shone on the young, musical world, Adam yawned. Eve yawned. The tight rhythms of Eve's chord progression and Adam's accompaniment took slack. Mistakes were made, but neither musician cared.

Finally, the music stopped altogether. The Landlord took a deep breath as Adam and Eve crawled into the trees and fell asleep in each others arms.

~~~

Adam and Eve awakened with hangovers the following afternoon. A few days later they were asked to leave the Garden for good. It seems Adam had hooked up iced tea glasses to amplifiers and had been playing them at outrageous volumes.

On her way out of the Garden into the Wilderness, Eve picked a piece of bark off a tree, a tree Adam had previously named the boo boo tree. She chewed on the sweet bark as she walked. Then, before she knew it, she was holding the reed-like thing between her teeth and blowing and drawing.

What a strange sound that piece of vibrating bark made! It sounded almost like a duck. *Wa! Wo! Wa!*

Adam turned to Eve. "What's that?" he asked. "What are those sounds?"

Eve only smiled.

Notes

* The NOTE is the basic unit of music.

* Notes form SCALES. If the first note of the scale is a **C**, this is a **C** scale. If the first note is a **G**, it's a **G** scale.

* When played at the same time, the 1st, 3rd and 5th notes of a scale HARMONIZE to form a MAJOR CHORD. The 1st, 3rd and 5th notes of a **C** scale play a **C** major chord. Likewise for an **A** or a **B** scale.

* The structure of most rock, blues and country western music is built around the I-IV-V CHORD PROGRESSION.

* Moving from one chord to the next forms a CYCLE. The I chord is the HOME BASE, the place where the music usually starts and ends. The IV chord moves the music further away from home base. The V chord moves it further still. Being away from home creates MUSICAL TENSION. Returning home RESOLVES THE TENSION.

* There are many VARIATIONS to the above cycle, but the I-IV-V progression is the foundation on which they're based.

* A simple way to ACCOMPANY another instrument playing the I-IV-V chord progression (or a variation) is to play musical patterns that emphasize the 1st, 3rd and 5th notes of the I chord's scale. No matter what chord the music plays, these HARMONIZING NOTES will not make a mistake.

* This accompaniment can sound BLUESY by including the $2\frac{1}{2}$ note of the I chord's major scale.

* This accompaniment can sound bluesy by including the $2\frac{1}{2}$, $4\frac{1}{2}$, and $6\frac{1}{2}$ notes of the I chord's major scale. In modern musical parlance, these numbers are called SCALE DEGREES and the blues notes are called the "flatted 3rd," the "flatted 5th" and "flatted 7th."

* It's natural to wonder how this fits in. Stay with me.

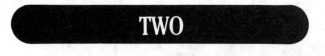

TWO

First Sounds of the Harmonica

Now that you have an idea how music is organized, it's time to pull out your harmonica and start making your own sounds. In Chapter II, you'll meet the world's first rock band, The Cave Boys, their harp player, Stone, and you will learn the harmonica essentials — what kind of harp to play, how to make your first sounds, and how to play chords and single notes.

Legend of the Cave Boys

From what little we know, the world's first rock band was a four person group called the Cave Boys. They played drums, bass, guitar and harmonica – amplifying their instruments through valuable electric tree stumps for which they had scoured the countryside.

The legend also tells us of Umm, the beautiful female vocalist who joined the Cave Boys and led them to stardom with such prehistoric hits as "Tango in the Tarpits" and "Funky Dinosaur."

The story that hasn't yet been told is that of Stone, the band's harmonica player. He started as a boy on a hillside with only the crickets and the coyotes for accompaniment. He went on to make the sweetest blues and rock harmonica sounds the world has ever heard.

What were Stone's secrets? How was he able to make that harmonica bend and warble with so much feeling – and always in perfect accompaniment to the band's pounding I-IV-V chord progression? How was he able to play bluesy sounding Cross Harp, then melodic Straight Harp, and finally exotic, minor key Slant Harp? Was he a human being or some bizarre musical god?

This story now belongs to you. All you need is a harmonica, a pair of lips, and a sense of fun. Dig it. Stone didn't know a lot about music, but he knew how to play it. As you're about to discover, you can play it too.

What Model of Harmonica?

To play blues, rock or country western harmonica in the modern age, you need a 10-hole DIATONIC* HARMONICA. While there are over 30 models available, these are a few of my favorites.

Hohner Marine Band–Here's the most popular harmonica in the world. Its basic design was created in 1896. True, the  wooden mouthpiece is a bit harder to play. The wood might swell, can be hard to slide across the lips–yet the old M.B. provides the warmest tone and is the favorite of those tough-lipped Chicago Blues players.

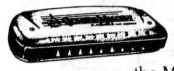 **Hohner Golden Melody**–This is a professional instrument that emphasizes technical clarity and precise tuning. Some feel it lacks the warmth of the Marine Band, possibly because of "equal tuning." Many feel it is the easiest harp for overblows. (See pages 206-208).

Lee Oskar–Designed and manufactured by one of our greatest players, Lee Oskar, the easy-playing and sweet-toned "Oskie" offers replacement reedplates (see page 210). The Oskar also comes in alternate tunings that are worth checking out. These include Harmonic Minor, Natural Minor and Melody Maker.

Hohner Special 20–This wonderful little harmonica is shaped like an M.B., but uses a plastic comb instead of a wooden one. The  result is a sweet-toned, easily-cupped blues harp, the favorite of millions.

Hohner Big River–At a smaller price, the Big River might be the easiest playing of all. It's an excellent instrument gaining in popularity.

Hohner Pocket Pal–This is a starter harmonica sold at one-fourth the price of the pro models listed above. While it sounds pretty good, the action is often more difficult. I usually recommend an upgrade for beginners because anything that makes harping easier is worth it.

If this is your first harmonica, the key of C is recommended.

*Diatonic: musical term referring to the do-re-mi-type scale.

A Closer Look

Stone's harmonicas were carefully carved from the tusk of wild boar with reeds fashioned from the hard bark of the boo boo tree. There are only a few of these harps in existence today. Of course, they're priceless.

The rest of us play harmonicas with nickle plated covers, wood or plastic air chambers, and brass reeds.

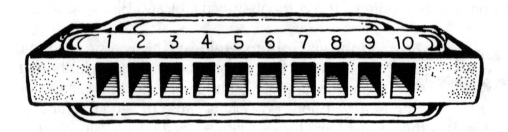

From 1 through 10, each air chamber (or hole) is numbered. Inside each air chamber are two reeds: thin strips of metal of different lengths. The reed on the ceiling of the air chamber vibrates when air is BLOWN through the harmonica. The reed on the floor of the chamber responds when air is sucked or DRAWN through the harp.

The reeds are sensitive, and well-directed shifts in air pressure and flow can alter the pitch of the tone. This is called BENDING.

On holes 1 through 6, blow notes are lower than draw notes. The situation reverses itself on holes 7 through 10. Up here draw notes are lower than blow notes.

When this book refers to, say, 4 draw, it means suck on hole 4. Four blow, or *4 blow*, means to blow on hole 4. In the charts and graphs, the number 4 with a circle around it means 4 draw. An uncircled 4 means 4 blow.

Here are some additional facts about your harmonica:

* The key of your harp is etched on its right end. If you own a **C** harp, 1 blow plays a **C** note. On a **D** harp, 1 blow is a **D** note.

* When playing, the key of your harmonica and the numbers identifying each hole should be facing up.

* The only complete scale on the reeds of your harmonica goes from 4 blow through 7 blow. Holes 1 through 4, and 7 through 10 have "missing notes." This setup allows you to play blow and draw chords on the low end of the harp and melodies on the top. Through bending, you can coax the "missing" notes out of the reeds.

Lay Out of Notes on C Harp

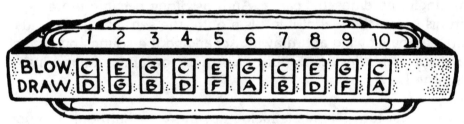

* Almost all the notes on your harp can be expressed in octaves. For instance, 1 draw is the same note as 4 draw and 8 draw. They are simply an octave apart. One blow is the same note as 4 blow and 7 blow. Three blow is the same note as 6 blow and 9 blow.

* From **G** (your lowest harp) through **F** sharp (your highest harmonica), the 12 different keyed harmonicas are organized exactly the same. If, by playing 6 blow, 5 draw, 4 draw, 4 blow, 3 draw, 3 blow, you can play a blues scale on your **G** harp, this same pattern of blows and draws will play a blues scale on your **F** sharp harmonica.

The only difference is that your **G** harp's blues scale will be very low in tone, and the blues scale on your **F** sharp harmonica will be quite high. This is the PRINCIPLE OF HARMONICA RELATIVITY: although they play in different keys, all harps have the same relationships of notes, scales and chords.

The Principle of Harmonica Relativity is both a convenience and a hassle. The hassle is that you need to carry around a number of different key harmonicas, and you never seem to have the one you need. The convenience is that you only have to learn a blues riff (pattern of notes) once to play it all different keys.

Playing Chords

Even Stone had to start somewhere.

The first sounds he made on his harmonica were rough and uncontrolled. "Will you shut up?" his father would yell as the young harp player sat in the corner of the cave and practiced. "You're going to attract dinosaurs!"

Amazingly, no dinosaurs came. And, as Stone became more familiar with his harp – the feel of it in his mouth, the sensation of sounds produced by blowing and drawing, changing the sounds by changing the shape of his lips and mouth – his music became admired instead of scorned.

Now it's your turn. Numbers facing up, put your harmonica to your lips. Make your mouth big enough to cover holes 1, 2, 3 and 4 at the same time. You may want to stretch a finger across holes 5, 6, 7, 8, 9 and 10 so you know where holes 1, 2, 3 and 4 are.

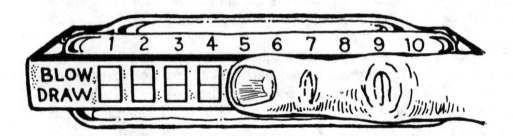

Keeping your mouth relaxed, blow gently into holes 1, 2, 3 and 4. Excellent! You've just played a major chord, the combination of 1-3-5 harmonizing notes that were discovered by Adam and Eve.

To play another major chord, draw on holes 1, 2, 3, 4. Listen as you play. This draw chord is higher than the blow chord. By going back and forth between the draw chord and the blow chord, you can play a simple two chord harmonica jam.

After you've explored the blows and draws of holes 1, 2, 3 and 4, slide the harp up one hole so you're playing 2, 3, 4 and 5. Blow and draw and move the harp up another hole to 3, 4, 5 and 6. Blow

38

and draw. Listen to the sounds of your harmonica. Make your breathing gentle and controlled as you slide the harp from one end to the other.

Some tips on moving the harmonica and playing chords:

1. Move the harp, not your head.

2. To make sure you're including hole number 1, place the low end of your harp in the corners of your lips.

3. If your chords have a bleating, forced quality, your mouth is too tight on the harp. Relax. Don't force the sounds. Clenching the harmonica between your teeth and blowing and drawing will give you an idea of how rich and full these chords can sound.

Along with its role as poster child for cosmetic dentistry, this illustration conveys the idea of keeping your mouth loose

Make your mouth loose.

4. When blowing, let air escape over the top of your harp. This will improve your tone, keep you from running out of breath, and lighten the air pressure on the reeds.

With these suggestions in mind, continue exploring the sounds of your harmonica. Make your playing slow and lazy. Learn to relax when the harmonica is in your mouth.

Stomping

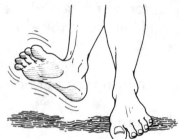

Stoneage drum machine

As you blow and draw your way up and down your harmonica, begin stomping a beat on the floor. Make this beat slow and steady. Count "1 – 2 – 1 – 2" or "1 – 2 – 3 – 4 – 1 – 2 – 3 – 4." Playing to a beat will give meaning and feeling to the sounds you make on your harp.

You can also get a beat by listening to the mechanical hum of a washing machine, the clicking and slurping of windshield wipers, the dripping of a faucet, or the busy signal on a telephone. Metronomes, drum machines, drum records and even real live drummers have been known to work. The important thing is to play to a beat.

Tonguing

Make a long blow or draw sound on your harp. Now flick the tip of your tongue – as though you were saying *ta ta ta* – on the ridge behind your upper teeth.

This *ta ta ta* tonguing action will stop and start the air traveling through your harp. This will stop and start the sound of your harp. The result is total control of a crisp, rhythmic harp sound. Now you can play your blows and draws for four, eight, or sixteen beats each, and by tonguing quickly, make the harp sound as though you were playing fast enough to beat the devil.

But *fast* is not the only form of rhythm. Making some sounds long and others short as in *taaaaa ta* or *tata taaaaa taaaaaa* is also very effective.

Spend a few minutes using your tongue to put rhythm into your impromptu harp music. DO NOT stop your breath when you tongue. Keep the air flow moving and let your tongue play the percussion.

40

Train Jam

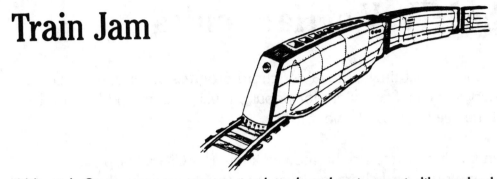

Although Stone never saw a train, he played train music like nobody's business. The harp sounds like a train when it huffs and puffs, builds up speed, goes faster and faster, and then, with the next station in view, slowly comes to a halt.

You can play train music (sometimes called Freight Harp) by going back and forth between the 1234 draw chord and the 1234 blow chord, giving each chord 1 beat. This is a I to IV chord jam.

(1234)	1234	(1234)	1234	(1234)
Draw	Blow	Draw	Blow	Draw
I	IV	I	IV	I

Start slowly, like a train leaving the station. Draw. Blow. Draw. Blow. Gradually go faster, letting air escape over the top of your harp on the blow chords.

Once your train is chugging down the track, you may want to try making a whistle sound. Draw holes 45 for eight beats, making these two notes cry out like the whistle of a train.

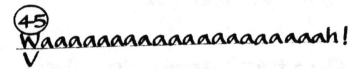

Without hesitating, return to your 1234 draw and blow pattern, playing the draw chord *before* you blow. Now, begin slowing down, like a train that knows the station is only a mile away.

Slower still, Chugalug, chugalug, chugalug on your 1234 draw and 1234 blow.

And finally, bring your train into the station, home at last.

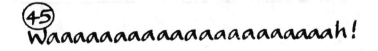

41

The I-IV-V of Harmonica

Since the earliest times, the I-IV-V chord progression or blues cycle has served as the framework for popular music. Adam and Eve used it. Stone used it. Now it's your turn.

When playing the style of harmonica known as Cross Harp (see the next chapter), your I chord is played by drawing on holes 1, 2, 3 and 4. Because the I chord is where the music usually starts and ends, it's called the CHORD OF RESOLUTION.

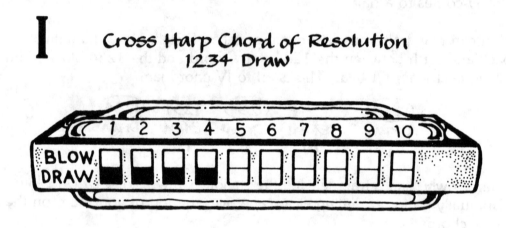

The IV chord can be played by blowing on holes 1, 2, 3 and 4. The IV chord moves the music away from the Chord of Resolution. It's called the STEPPING STONE CHORD.

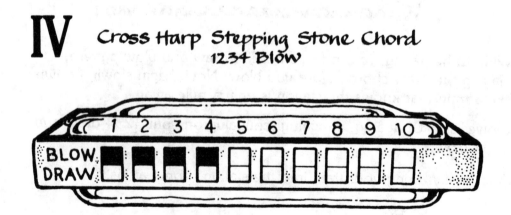

The V chord can be played by drawing on holes 4, 5 and 6.
The V chord creates musical tension, and you can think of it as
the DOMINANT WAILER CHORD.

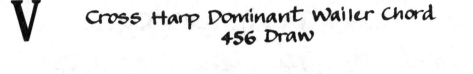

To play a simple I-IV-V chord progression, begin stomping your foot
1-2-1-2.* Once you've got a beat going, play the Cross Harp Chord
of Resolution for two stomps. Play the Stepping Stone Chord for
two stomps. Play the Dominant Wailer Chord for two stomps.
Complete your blues cycle by returning to the Chord of Resolution.
Then play the cycle again.

Want to Sound More Musical?

Start a stomach tremble, a vibration from deep in your body that
gives your breath and harmonica sound a pulse. Think of this as a
tremolo or vibrato—a soft vibrating pressure from your gut. This
vibrato can go soft or hard, slow or fast. At first, it's easier on the
blow, but soon this tremolo will be a part of how you play.

---

* How fast should you stomp? Try pulse speed. Place your thumb on the big
vein of your wrist. Feel the rhythm of your heartbeat. The first beat is 1, the
second is 2, the third is 1 and so on. Start stomping at the same speed. Other
ideas are to use a metronome or drum machine.

I-IV-V Beginner's Cycle

(1234) Resolution I   1234 Stepping IV   (456) Wailing V   (1234) Resolution I

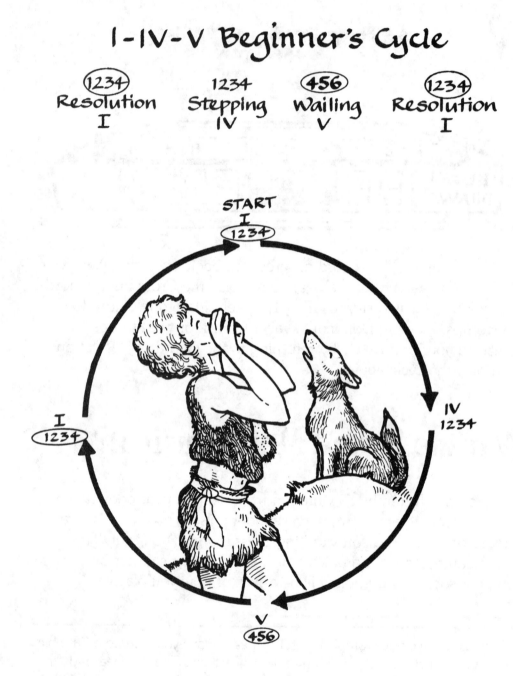

You can add rhythm and meaning by tonguing every chord twice.

You can change the order of chords in a I-IV-V progression. The next chord cycle plays the Dominant Wailer V Chord BEFORE the Stepping Stone IV Chord.

Foot Stomper's Cycle

(1234) Resolution I   (456) Wailing V   1234 Stepping IV   (1234) Resolution I

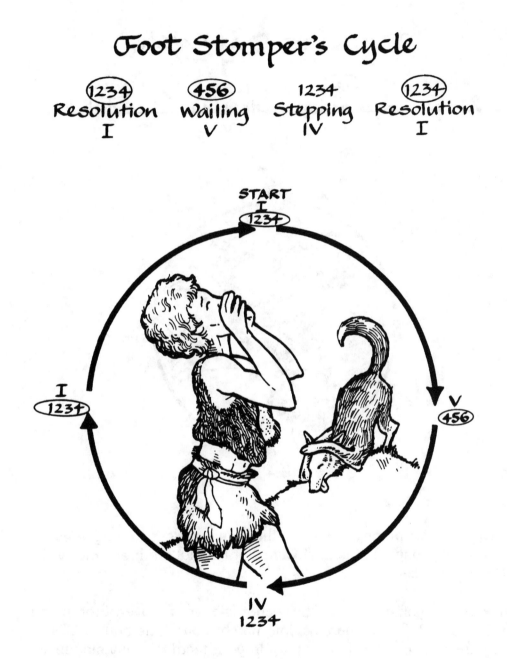

After you've played the above chord cycle a few times without tonguing, tongue every chord three times each time you bring your foot down (this is called a triplet). Not tonguing the final Chord of Resolution will add to the sense of completion.

The next chord cycle starts on the Dominant Wailer and ends on the Chord of Resolution.

Dancing Dog Cycle

(456)   (1234)   1234   (1234)
Wailer   Resolution   Stepping   Resolution
  V   I   IV   I

A suggestion for putting rhythm in the above cycle is to tongue every chord twice. Tonguing the final Chord of Resolution three times will add still more pzazzz.

Get a rhythm going and play these chords over and over. Stomp your foot 1-2-1-2-1-2. Play harp as you march around the house. Clap your hands as you clench your harp in your teeth. Do anything that will help you return to that ancient cave of your mind and that subterranean river where music and rhythm flow.

In other words, get it on!

Let's Learn to Play Single Notes

The most important skill in harping is playing one note at a time–single notes. Both puckering and tongue-blocking, two important approaches for blues and rock harp, follow **Rule #1: Put the harp as deeply as possible in your mouth.** At first, this seems harder. But remember, the goal is to make your body and the harmonica one musical instrument. While learning, you need to focus on where and how the harp and body connect. Where? At the inner lips. How? Through the air that moves through the harp, through the tunnel your pushed-out lips form, into your body.

Rule #2: If you hold the harp on the edge of your lips, your tone will be lousy. (Guaranteed)

Rule #3: If your lips are clamped tightly on the harp, or your throat is constricted, your tone will be lousy. (Also guaranteed)

If you are just starting out, I recommend the pucker or lip-blocking method. Begin on 4 draw. Take a look at the hole and resolve to play it for six or seven seconds. Place the harmonica between your **inner lips**–as though you are going to play a big chord. Now, pushing your lips out, narrow the opening into the harp and draw in a controlled, pressurized column of air.

A proper single note feels good to play physically. Overtones and sympathetic vibrations resonate in your ears and body. It feels so good, you want to play harp all the time. Using back pressure, compression and resistance, you add vibrato, tone color and pitch changes. It all starts here with how you put the harmonica in your mouth.

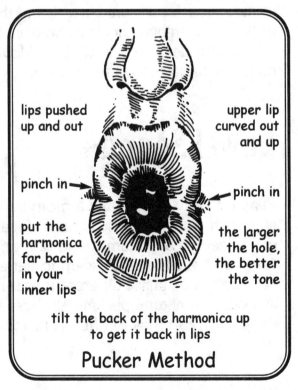

lips pushed up and out

upper lip curved out and up

pinch in →

← pinch in

put the harmonica far back in your inner lips

the larger the hole, the better the tone

tilt the back of the harmonica up to get it back in lips

Pucker Method

Inner Compression

One of the greatest secrets of harmonica tone is **inner compression**. The trick is to pressurize a column of air as it enters and leaves and stays in your body. You do this by slightly resisting the airstream at your lips–and everywhere else.

This resistance creates a **back pressure**, a sense that the tissues of your body are filled with air. This back pressure starts at the stomach and forms the air column all the way to your lips, both blow and draw. You know you have compression and back pressure if (without the harmonica) your airstream makes a loud and long hissing sound you can draw for 10 seconds.

Reverse,
Control
and Shape
Airstream

Whether
Blowing
or Drawing,

Always
Push
From
Here

Vibrato Against Compression

If you tremble against the compression at your stomach, you get a beautiful **vibrato**. If you move the focus of the trembling to your throat, you get a different vibrato of different intensity. The secret is to create back pressure by resisting the note, then tremble against this pressure. Trembling against the back pressure in your stomach produces a deep rumbly vibrato. Moving the trembling to the throat makes for a faster, lighter vibrato.

Vowel Sounds
A E I O U

Play a 3 blow. If you take a moment to softly say "oo" as in cool while you push your trembling stomach against your body's own resistance, you'll feel the airstream round out, and so will your tone. If you say "ee," that airstream will seem to flatten out tonewise. That is because "ee" and "oo" utilize different throat muscles. The "oo" pushes your lips out in a natural pucker. All these factors affect the most important thing your harp has to offer–your tone.

Articulating   ta   ka   ya
da   wa

People who pucker for their single notes usually use the "ta ta" (or perhaps "to to") action described on page 40 to create notes of different lengths and intensity. Tonguing is effective for imitating the cadences of speech, locomotives, and also for playing clean musical passages. Try tonguing the syllables below as though the harp were a blues singer.

④   •   •   •   •   •   ③ ②

"My   baby left me this morning!

④   •   •   •   •   4 ③ ②
Now I'm as sad as I can be"

◯ = Draw   • = Articulate (ta, ka, or wa)

Three blow and 2 draw are the same notes.
Use 3 blow if 2 draw is a problem for you.

If you use tongue-blocking for single notes, it is difficult to use the tongue to articulate because it is so busy blocking out air on the harmonica. In order to articulate notes, use the "Ka" sound. This clicking in your throat can create effective articulations. So can an air-bursting "Ha" sound that's fueled by pushing from your stomach.

You can also use the wa wa wa action of your hands to articulate notes. You can also use bending.

Notes of Different Lengths

When first practicing your single notes, you should play notes that last two or four beats. To get a feel for that, just snap your fingers a few times. Each time you snap–that's a quarter note. If you snap two times at each beat, you're snapping out 8th notes. If you jam in four quick snaps on each beat, you've got 16th notes.

Going in the other direction, if you play a long unbroken harmonica note that covers four snaps or stomps, that's called a whole note, and a half note last two beats.

49

Tongue-blocking

There is another very important approach to playing the harmonica–a technique called tongue-blocking. The idea is to play chords–with a big open mouth–and use your tongue to block out every hole but the one you want to play.

As shown below, play 1234 draw and use the tip of your tongue to cover holes 123 so only hole 4 plays.

Attach harp here

Tongue-blocking Method

Or, if you want to get fancy about it, play **octaves**. For instance, make your mouth big enough to play holes 1234 draw. Block out holes 2 and 3 so holes 1 and 4 draw play. These are two **D** notes, an octave apart, playing at the same time. You can move this embouchure all over the harmonica and get this effect.

Another technique is called **the tongue-slap**. If you are tongue-blocking a single note at 4 draw on holes 1234, and quickly lift and replace your tongue, you get a quick rhythmic burst, a shadow of a chord behind your single note 4 draw. You can use this as a form of rhythmic articulation, and also as a way of shadowing your single note, having the power of a full chord behind it.

The Octave

Many people argue about which is better, tongue-blocking or puckering. For the heavy Little Walter* sound, tongue-blocking is essential. It allows a complexity that simple puckering does not.

*Walter Jacobs, grandfather of modern electric blues harp.

50

Practicing Single Notes

This is the part of the book that involves YOU. Pick a note–say 4 draw, as your practice note. Now wait–don't start yet. First, **hear** a clear, pure, rich harmonica tone in your mind. It's always important to try to hear what it is you want to play. As for these funky diagrams, to me they represent columns of air.

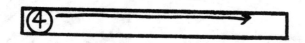

1. Practice your single notes for at least 4 beats so you have a chance to adjust your embouchure and airstream for the best results.

2. Whether tongue-blocking or puckering, play with the harp as connected to your body (deep in your mouth) as possible.

3. Whether puckering or tongue-blocking, play with a totally relaxed embouchure.

4. Include the vowel sounds "ee" and "oo" as you play clear round single notes, and actively listen for tonal changes.

5. Connect your body to the harp with back pressure–putting the air under a state of compression.

6. Think air control: make each pull and push smooth, strong and gentle.

7. Use as little air as possible. Instead use back pressure and muscular resistance to increase the amplitude of the air.

8. Think vibrato: push from your stomach whether blowing or drawing.

9. Think articulation: whole and half notes, quarter notes, eighths, sixteenths.
   Puckerers use ta.
   Tongue-blockers use ka.

51

THREE

Second Position Cross Harp– Style of the Blues

Cross Harp is the style of harmonica that plays blues. It involves accenting the draw notes instead of the blow notes and playing a C harp in the key of G. Now learn how and why it works.

First Position* "Straight Harp"
C Harp in the Key of C

After about a year of tooting mindlessly on his boo boo reed harmonica, Stone realized that there were two basic harmonica styles: STRAIGHT HARP, with its accent on the BLOW, and it's bluesy cousin CROSS HARP, with its accent on the DRAW.

Straight Harp was the type of music that played old melodies, the kind his mother sang to him when he was a child. Later this style became popular for playing Civil War songs, cowboy songs, Bible songs.

Straight Harp works like this: If you blow on holes 1234 of your **C** harp, you play a **C** chord. In fact, just about anywhere you blow three or more notes, bottom, middle or top of the harmonica, you'll get a **C** chord. Your **C** notes are located at single notes 1, 4, 7 and 10 blow.

Harken back to the story of Adam and Eve and how each chord was made up of 1-3-5 harmonizing notes and that these harmonizing notes wouldn't make a mistake when jamming. When playing Straight Harp, **C** harp in the key of **C**, **every blow note is a harmonizing note**. This, of course, is why you play Straight Harp with accent on the blow.

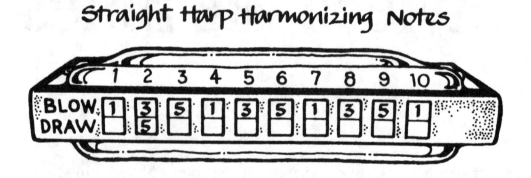

Every blow note harmonizes. Every draw note makes it interesting. See my book *Harmonica Americana* to learn great straight harp melodies.

*Why is it called 1st position? Because we're playing C harp in the key of C. That's the simple answer. The complicated answer is on page 200.

As you practice your single notes, try the 1st position "do-re-mi" scale. Before playing it, try singing it or hearing it in your mind. It's always a good idea to try to hear what you want to play before playing it.

4 ④ 5 ⑤ 6 ⑥ ⑦ 7
do re mi fa so la ti do

While Straight Harp is not used that often in rock and blues harmonica styles, it is the first style most people usually learn. That's because it's so easy and natural to play with a push/pull/push breath pattern, and because the old songs are relatively easy to play. Give this post-primitive classic a try.

Red River Valley   C harp in key of C

3 4 5 • • • ④ 5 ④ 4
From this valley they say you are leaving

3 4 5 4 5 6 ⑤ 5 ④
We will miss your bright eyes and sweet smile

6 ⑤ 5 • ④ 4 ④ 5 6 ⑤
For they say you have taken the sunshine   ◯ = Draw

3 • • ③ 4 ④ 5 ④ 4
That has brightened our lives for awhile   • = Tongue or
                                                  Articulate

This is a great first song for anyone to learn. You can utilize the tongue-blocking or single note embouchure, and articulate the syllables of the words by tonguing, use of hands, bending, or by other means such as "ka ka" or tongue-slapping. You can also play octaves on many of the notes.

How to begin: first, hear the song in your mind. Then seek out the notes, slowly. Make the articulation of the harp match the words of the song. Create a slow body rhythm that goes 1-2-3-1-2-3, and play the melody over it.

Cross Harp: Second Position
C Harmonica in the Key of G

To understand Cross Harp, the style of the blues, go back to Adam and Eve. Eve lined up a musical instrument of waterglasses in the **C** scale and played music in the key of **C**. Second position, or Cross Harp, is the style you get when you play that same musical **C** instrument (in this case a harmonica) in the key of **G**.

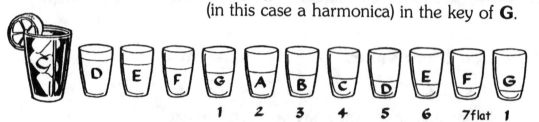

The reason you play a **C** harp in the key of **G** is that if you draw on holes 1234 at the same time, you get a **G** chord. The draw notes are the blues notes, the notes you can really wail on and bend.

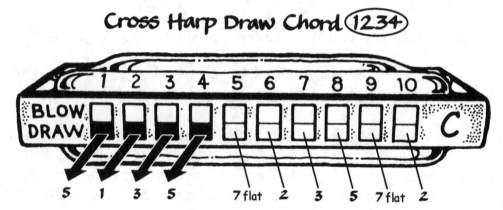

As shown on page 42, when you play holes 1 through 4 draw at the same time, you get the I chord. Played one at a time, these single notes—at 1 draw, 2 draw, 3 draw and 4 draw—create the structure of your blues riffs, and will get you through almost any chord progression in the key of **G**. These are HARMONIZING NOTES, notes that won't make a mistake. As mentioned, they are also the notes you can bend.

Check out "Swing Low, Sweet Chariot." Notice how you play mostly the low draw notes, and glide over the blows. This is a good example of how Cross Harp works. At this point, 3 draw and 2 draw may present special problems. Think of this song as an example of Cross Harp, not a requirement for the first day's reading.

SWING LOW, SWEET CHARIOT–2nd position

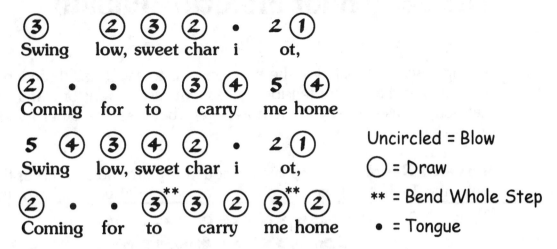

Uncircled = Blow
◯ = Draw
** = Bend Whole Step
• = Tongue

Creating and Resolving Tension

Musical tension is the feeling the music is crying out for something. That *something* is a feeling of resolution, a sense that the music has arrived home. As a general rule, create tension by fearlessly holding certain notes or chords–like the 3 draw (above), 4 draw (above), 5 draw, 6 draw–against the beat. Resolve the tension on the 2 draw (above) or 3 blow or 6 blow, the **G** notes on your **C** harp. Use the notes between, mostly blow notes, as stepping stones.

2nd Position G Scales for the C Harp

There are many different blues scales. Here are two that avoid bends. Along with learning songs and working on techniques, scales make good practice as you develop your single note, harp-moving skills.

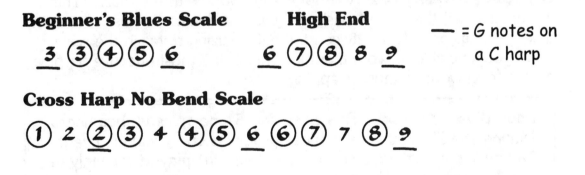

Bending is described on page 116. It is not necessary to accomplish now.

The Search for Musical Tension

A simple way of looking at the harmonica is to say it has three kinds of notes. Notes that create tension. Notes that resolve tension. And notes that you use as stepping stone notes–steps between the other two kinds of notes.

Notes of Resolution resolve tension. They are the root note, the tonic, the 1st note of the key you're playing in. On your C harp, they are G notes.

Cross Harp Notes of Resolution
2 Draw, 3 Blow, 6 Blow, 9 Blow

Wailing Notes create tension. You can use them as harmonizers, notes that won't make a mistake. As you play them, emphasizing them, making them drag on and on, you create a sense of musical expectation. Plus, as the music continues from one chord to the next, Wailing Notes will, for the most part, adjust.

Cross Harp Wailing Notes
1 Draw, 3 Draw, 4 Draw, 5 Draw, 6 Draw, 7 Draw, 8 Draw, 9 Draw, 10 Draw

Stepping Stone Notes will not always work with the music. There are times when they might clash. At first, you'll learn to pass over them quickly, rungs on ladder between the harmonizing notes in the scale. Later you'll be able to work them in. In fact, the most effective harping comes from working those Stepping Notes.

Four Blow Warning!!! This Stepping Stone trips up beginners. During the IV part of the blues progression, it sounds great. In the V part, it can also be effective. But played strongly in the I chord, it can be a dead-end clunker that changes the direction of the song and can mess you up, big time.

Map of Cross Harp

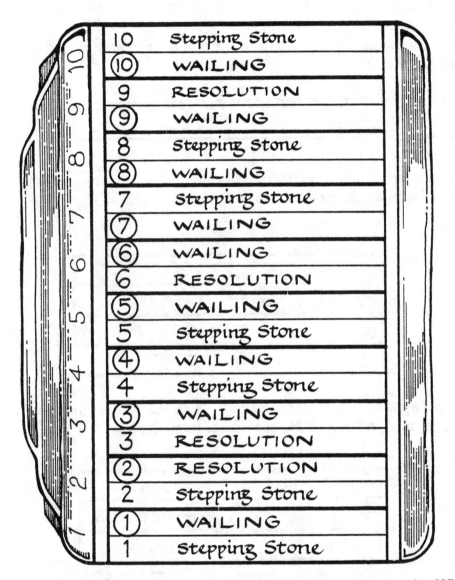

10	Stepping Stone
⑩	WAILING
9	RESOLUTION
⑨	WAILING
8	Stepping Stone
⑧	WAILING
7	Stepping Stone
⑦	WAILING
⑥	WAILING
6	RESOLUTION
⑤	WAILING
5	Stepping Stone
④	WAILING
4	Stepping Stone
③	WAILING
3	RESOLUTION
②	RESOLUTION
2	Stepping Stone
①	WAILING
1	Stepping Stone

Notes of Resolution resolve musical tension when playing solo. When used to accompany a blues band playing a I-IV-V (or other) progression, they temporarily become Wailing Notes during the IV and V. When the band returns to the I chord, Notes of Resolution resolve the tension.

Wailing Notes create musical tension. You can bend the notes at 1 draw, 3 draw, 4 draw and 6 draw, increasing the tension. (page 116) Wailing Notes at 5 draw, 7 draw, 8 draw, 9 draw and 10 draw don't bend and are not as versatile their bending brothers.

Stepping Stone Notes, when emphasized, tend to change the direction of the song–unless you play them at exactly the right moment. This is why you usually tread lightly on these notes.

59

First Boogie

Tap out a 3 blow on your harp. Stomp your foot and loosen up. That's right....

Now move that harp a tiny bit and draw on hole 4. Tongue that baby. Create a little tension. Hold that note as you stomp 1-2-1-2-1-2.

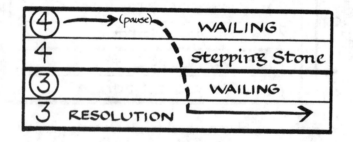

Now pause. *Feel* the tension you've created. Dig the silence. Now, and only now, play your Note of Resolution, 3 blow.

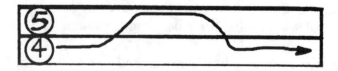

Oh yeah! Establish home base. Create tension. Resolve tension. Stomp your foot. Get down. Do it again. Whew! Play a long 4 draw to the 1-2-1-2 beat. Slide up to 5 draw, back to 4 draw.

From your wailing 4 draw, blow on hole 4, wail on the 3 draw, holding that note out, creating tension, and resolve on the 3 blow.

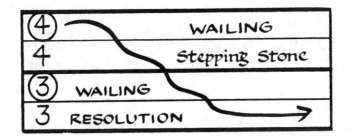

What a sound! *Stress* those harmonizing notes. Glide over those Stepping Stones.

Tongue that 3 blow. Create tension on 3 draw. Resolve on 3 blow. Keep your rhythm going....

Play a long, wailing 6 draw. *Ta ta ta, ta ta ta, ta ta ta.*

Resolve your tension on 6 blow.

Oh yeah! Get down and loosen up! You've got the blues in your shoes. Play 'em.

The Cross Harp Formula

The Cross Harp formula is a simple way to choose the correct key harmonica when playing Cross Harp to accompany a guitarist or piano player.

Ask the guitarist what key the song is in. If the answer is **G**, count up four steps (including the **G**)...

$$
\begin{array}{cccc}
G & A & B & C \\
1 & 2 & 3 & 4
\end{array}
$$

...and play your **C** harp in the key of **G**.

Likewise, if you have a **C** harp, and want to tell the guitarist what key to play in, count *back* four steps from the **C**. (It's okay to use your fingers!)

$$
\begin{array}{cccc}
G & A & B & C \\
4 & 3 & 2 & 1
\end{array}
$$

Here is a chart that tells you which harmonica you need to play Cross Harp in each of music's twelve different keys.

Musical Key	Key of Harp for Cross Harp
A flat	D flat
A	D
B flat	E flat
B	E
C	F
D flat	F sharp
D	G
E flat	A flat
E	A
F	B flat
F sharp	B
G	C

HOW TO FIGURE THE CROSS HARP FORMULA.

Notes

* There are two basic styles of harmonica playing: STRAIGHT HARP and CROSS HARP.

* Straight Harp accents the blow notes. When you play your **C** harmonica in the key of **C**, you are playing Straight Harp. Straight Harp works best for melodic harmonica.

* Cross Harp emphasizes the harmonica's draw notes. This blues harmonica style lets you play your **C** harmonica in the key of **G**.

* There are two kinds of notes on your harmonica: HARMONIZING NOTES and STEPPING STONES. Accompanying a I-IV-V chord progression, harmonizing notes will never make a mistake— no matter where in the progression they are played.

* There are two kinds of harmonizing notes: WAILING NOTES and NOTES OF RESOLUTION. Notes of Resolution establish home base and resolve tension. Wailing Notes move the music away from home base and create tension.

* To play bluesy patterns of notes (also known as riffs, runs, and licks), emphasize Wailing Notes and Notes of Resolution. Use non-harmonizing Stepping Stone Notes as links between these Wailers and Resolvers.

* To figure out which key of harmonica to use when playing Cross Harp, find out what key the music is in. If the music you're accompanying is in, say, the key of **A** count up four steps...

A B C D
1 2 3 4

...and play a **D** harp.

FOUR

Cave Jam: How to Accompany

Travel back 10,000 years to that musty cave where The Cave Boys are laying down some good tunes. Bring your harmonica and play some simple accompaniment. Hey, you play pretty good!

Cave Jam

It was a large, comfortable cave high in the hills above a broad valley. This was where the Cave Boys practiced. The sounds of their instruments would echo loudly off the cave walls. But because the cave was far away from the homes of other cave men, there were few complaints about noise.

It was Sunday afternoon, and the Cave Boys were getting ready to play. This was a new song, written by Krok, the band's lead guitar player and singer. The song was in the key of **G**.*

Counting up four steps, **G** (1) **A** (2) **B** (3) **C** (4), Stone was prepared to boogie on his **C** harp.

Krok's fingers formed a **G** chord on his guitar. "You guys ready?" he asked.

"Yeah," said the big drummer, Smash.

Gref, the bass player, nodded. Stone softly tapped his **C** harp in the palm of his hand.

"Okay," said Krok, "One-two-three-four!"

Whang bam thump thump! The I-IV-V chord progression started with 16 beats (1-2-3-4 played 4 times) in the key of **G**. This was the I chord, and established **G** as the home base for the tune.

As the sixteenth beat came down, Krok swung his guitar low across his body and changed his **G** chord to a **C** chord. This was the IV chord and the music stayed here for 8 beats. *Whamma bam bam!* slammed the drums as the music returned to the **G**, this time for 8 beats.

"Yeah!" shouted Smash, big arms flailing as he pounded his cymbals and snare drums.

Here in the **G**, the chord progression seemed be asking for a change, and a change is what it got. The Cave Boy guitarist nodded to his bass player, jumped lightly from the dirt cave floor and played a **D** chord, the Dominant Wailer V chord of the I-IV-V chord progression. This **D** chord gave the music a new feeling of movement, of going somewhere. The **D** lasted 4 beats. Then chord cycle swung down to the **C** chord for 4 tense beats. Oh, yeah!

Krok slammed down out the **G** chord as the blues cycle came home to the I chord. Four incredible beats passed and the cycle was almost complete. But what's this? With only 4 beats left in the blues cycle, Krok returned to to his Dominant Wailer, the **D** chord.

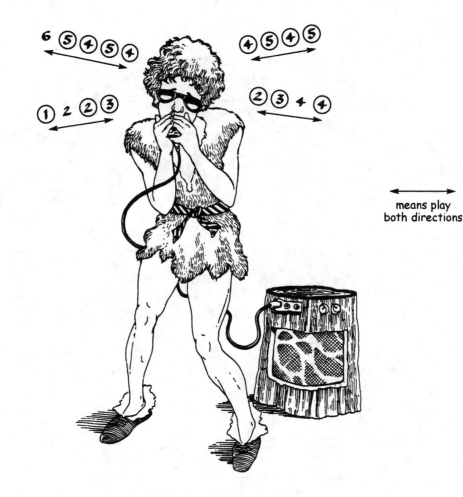

means play
both directions

"Turn it around!" shouted Smash. The tension wailed for 1-2-3-4 beats, and at exactly the right moment, the music dove home to the **G** chord for a dramatic resolution of the old cycle and the start of a new one.

This was the TWELVE BAR BLUES BLUES CYCLE, a special I-IV-V chord progression that even today is almost always heard when a band plays the slow blues. But Krok didn't care about that. He wanted to hear his harp player. "Come on, Stoney Boy!" he shouted. "Come on!"

Stone began by playing Wailing Note 4 draw. As the I-IV-V chord progression moved through its cycle, each chord change gave the 4 draw new meaning and feeling–almost as though he were changing notes. But because this wailing 4 draw was a harmonizing note, it never made a mistake.

Then, as the cycle neared resolution (and Stone's lungs were about to explode), the feisty harp player went to the Note of Resolution, 3 blow. The 3 blow and the I Chord of Resolution hit at exactly the same time. Wow!

Now, as the cycle started around again, Stone tongued his 3 blow Note of Resolution, *beating* a rhythm, *phrasing* his sounds the way a singer phrases words. Stone tongued this 3 blow through the entire cycle.

As the cycle started up once more, Stone began playing other Cross Harp harmonizing notes. He played the 6 draw Wailer. He took a run up to the 9 blow Note of Resolution and played his harp down, curling over the notes to Note of Resolution 3 blow. Because he accented the Notes of Resolution and Wailing Notes and played the Stepping Stone Notes lightly, like rungs on a ladder between the harmonizers, he never made a mistake.

"Alright!" shouted Stone as the cycle came to a close. The guitarist opened his mouth wide and started to sing. He might not have had the best voice in the world, but when it came to grunting, groaning, moaning and screaming, no one did it better, or looked cooler.

G *(guitar chords)*
"I've got the Cave Boy Blues, and wouldn't it be fine?"

G
(Stone tongued his 3 blow for 8 beats)

C

"I've got the Cave Boy blues, and wouldn't it be fine?"

G
(Stone played 3 blow, moved to 4 draw and wailed for 8 beats)

D   **C**   **G**
"If you'd pay a little visit to Krokie boy's cave sometime."

G   **D**   **G**
(Stone tongued 3 blow, wailed on 4 draw, slid up to 6 draw, resolved on 6 blow)

"Alright!" shouted Krok, sounding a little like a man with his leg caught in a meat grinder.

Now Stone played a solo of low notes. He drew and tongued hole number one. He blew on hole two and sucked a clear single note on Note of Resolution 2 draw.

His 2 draw slipped up to 3 draw. By changing the shape of his mouth and throat, Stone sucked that note deep into his gut. The 3 draw dipped down to a "bent" 3 draw.* This was the 2½ blues harmonizing note discovered by Adam. It sounded soooo good.

The blues cycle was coming around to the Dominant Wailer. Stone jumped up to holes 4 and 5 draw. These were the tension creating Wailing Notes, the single note expressions of the V Dominant Wailer Chord. Stone swivelled his harmonica back and forth between 4 and 5 draw without stopping his breath.

He continued this 4 and 5 single note draw slide through the IV chord, slipping the harp back and forth like a typewriter carriage between moist Cave Boy lips. It was a small subtle move, but what a sound it made!

Then, as the cycle came home, Stone came home to the 6 blow Note of Resolution. He played 6 draw as the cycle turned around with the Dominant Wailer V Chord, and blew home with a wild flurry of notes that somehow landed on the 3 blow at exactly the same moment that Krok dropped to his knees, clutched his guitar to his chest, and started to sing:

G
"I've got the Cave Boy blues, and wouldn't it be great?"

G
(Stone drew a long 3 draw bent down for 7 beats and played 3 blow on the 8th beat)

C
"I've got the Cave Boy blues and wouldn't it be great?"

---

* More about bending in Chapter VII

70

G
(Stone played 1 draw, 2 blow, 2 draw and made that 2 draw talk
until the 8th beat)

D   **C**   **G**
"If you'd consent to be this cave boy's date."

G   **D**   **G**
(Stone played 4 draw, 4 blow, 3 draw, 4 blow, 3 draw, 2 draw)

Stone caressed home his 2 draw Note of Resolution and took off
on a new solo. Smash double thumped his drums and Gref's low
bass notes drove home a deep blues feeling. Round and round went
the I-IV-V chord progression, this twelve bar blues cycle.
Stone's harmonica growled like a wildcat, howled like a coyote,
moaned like a lover who wanted more. It was incredible.

Stone even played the Six Blow Down, a harp riff using Adam's
Blues Scale – only in reverse. Note of Resolution 6 blow was the 1st
note. Five draw was the 6½ note. Four draw served as the wailing
5th note. Four blow was the 4th note. Three draw bent down was
the 2½ blues harmonizing note, and 3 blow, another Note of
Resolution, was the 1st note of the scale.

Blues Scale Down
6 ⑤ ④ 4 ③ 3

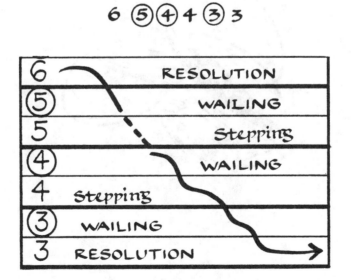

As the music swelled and reverberated off the musty walls, the other band members just looked at each other. Stone's music sounded so good it was hard to concentrate.

How could he do all that on a tiny harmonica?

Finally, Krok could stand it no longer. He put his guitar down, unplugged it from his electric tree stump. "Tell me..." he gasped, "Tell me...how did you do that?"

Stone smiled. "What key is the next song in?" Then he turned away and acted busy. A harp player never reveals his or her secrets — unless there's cash involved.

Finally, Stone agreed to teach the Cave Boys how to play Cross Harp for 20 clams a person. Fresh, *plump* clams. And he'd even let them use his harps.

Notes

* Music moves in circles. The circle almost always plays the same chord pattern again and again. This is a CHORD PROGRESSION. Most chord progressions are built around the I-IV-V pattern.

* To jam with a band, guitarist, or a record, find out where the music begins and ends. This is the KEY you're playing in.

* Select the CORRECT KEY HARMONICA. To play Cross Harp, count up 4 steps from the key the music is in. If the music is in the key of **G**, play a **C** harp. If the music is in the key of **E**, play an **A** harp.

* Get a FEEL for the music before you start your accompaniment. Let the rhythm flow through your body. Get a sense of the chord progression's circular motion.

* A good way to START YOUR ACCOMPANIMENT is to play a long 4 draw. Hear how each chord change gives new meaning and feeling to this harmonizing note.

* GO SLOW AND HAVE A GOOD TIME.

FIVE

Stone's Harmonica Lesson: Blues and Rock Riffs

Riffs are patterns of notes that always sound bluesy and musical. They connect Notes of Resolution, Wailing Notes and Stepping Stone Notes to help you make music as you blow and draw your way around the harmonica. Some of the riffs in Chapter V are too difficult to play immediately. Don't let this stop you from tooting along and having a good time.

The Lesson Begins

Stone told the Cave Boys how Wailing Notes create musical tension and Notes of Resolution resolve tension. He told them how Stepping Stone Notes were used as links, or rungs on a ladder, between Wailing Notes and Notes of Resolution. Still, the band was impatient.

"Okay," growled Smash. "Now we know which notes create tension and which notes resolve it. What are we supposed to do? Play them all at the same time?"

"Take it easy," said Stone. "Let's take Wailing Note 4 draw and Note of Resolution 3 blow. We know you can play either one – and they'll always work when you accompany a I-IV-V chord progression." He picked up his harmonica and played the Beginner's Blues Riff.

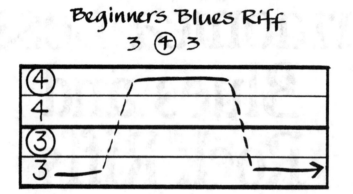

"If playing 3 blow and 4 draw always works, why not build a ladder, using 3 draw and 4 blow as Stepping Stones? Like this:"

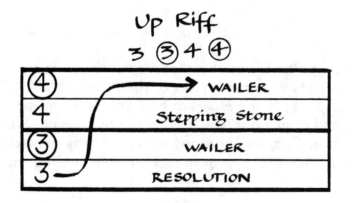

76

He handed each of the Cave Boys a small diatonic harmonica. "Now you guys try it...but don't spit too much in the harps. It clogs them up."

Each of the Cave Boys tried to play the Up Riff.

But instead of the smooth, rich tone Stone got from his harmonica, all the Cave Boys could produce was a cacophony of hisses, bleats, and honks.

It sounded like an invasion of geese.

"C'mon, you guys," said Stone. "You gotta get a good single note before you can play a lick. You gotta get a good soft mouth, like this."

He pushed his lips out so the the hole they formed a large, vertical oval.

"And see, you put the harmonica well inside your inner lips. Push the harp up a little bit, toward your nose, so the upper lip doesn't have to stretch so much and can cover half the upper plate of the harp."

He looked at Smash, whose face was set in a determined grimace. "Smash!" he shouted.

But it was too late. Smash removed the harmonica from his mouth. It was crushed to smithereens – bent by the pressure of the big drummer's clenched lips.

"You gotta relax!" shouted Stone. "You gotta mellow out with those big lips of yours!"

He looked sadly at the crushed harmonica.

"Okay," he finally sighed. "Let's try again. Blow and draw on hole 3; blow and draw on hole 4. Remember, 4 draw is your Wailing Note, so play the 3 blow, 3 draw and 4 blow quickly and smoothly. Then, when you get to the 4 draw, stretch it out. Waaaaaiiiillllllllll."

Once again the Cave Boys played the Up Riff. This time it sounded a lot better, though there were still many missed notes and strange honking sounds.

"That's a little better," said Stone. "But I don't see what's so hard about it. You blow and draw on 3. You blow and draw on 4, and you hold the 4 draw a long time to create tension."

The Cave Boys went at it again. Sure enough, they could hear the blues in this simple pattern of notes. In fact, a few of the times they tried it, even Stone was impressed. Of course, he didn't tell them.

Those crazy dudes might think they already know how to play harp. They might decide to forget about the lesson. And Stone could taste those clams.

The Down Riff

"Now that you're playing a riff that takes you up your harmonica, I'm gonna show you one that takes you down," said Stone. "All you've got to do is play the Up Riff in reverse. And dig it, you've got a hot blues lick."

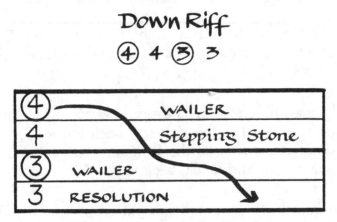

"That's it," Stone said as the Cave Boys played their own versions of the Down Riff.

"Now, 4 draw is a Wailing Note, so play it a long time. Maybe two beats, eh? The 4 blow is a Stepping Stone Note so play it quickly and move to the 3 draw. The 3 draw is a Wailer. You can really create tension with this little bugger, so hold it out. Try to create a sense of anticipation for the 3 blow. Then, after 2 or 3 beats (depending on how it feels best to you), play 3 blow."

"And the Down Riff is like the Up Riff? It will always sound good when accompanying a I-IV-V chord progression?" asked Krok.

"Of course," said Stone. "As long as it accents the Wailing Notes and Notes of Resolution."

"Prove it," said Krok. He picked up his guitar and began playing. His fingers leapt from chord to chord. First he played a **G** chord, then an **A minor** chord, then a **C** chord, and lastly, a **D** chord.

"Hey!" said Smash. "That's not a I-IV-V chord progression."

"Doesn't have to be a I-IV-V." said Stone. "As long as the music stays in the same key, these riffs will always work no matter how the song goes. All you have to do is *mold* them to the music."

As Krok strummed the chords, Stone played the Down Riff as fast as he could, over and over. It fit perfectly with the music.

Then he played it very slowly, putting a big accent on the 3 draw Wailing Note. Again, it sounded great with guitar music.

Next, Stone played the Down Riff so the 4 draw lasted 12 beats, the 4 blow and 3 draw occurred in 1 beat and the resolving 3 blow was played for 3 beats.

Now Krok changed his chord progression. He stayed in the key of **G**, but his fingers jumped to the **F** chord, back to the **G**, to the **F**, back to the **G**. Then he went to the **E** minor chord, the **A** minor chord, to the **D** chord, and finally back to the **G** chord.

"Whew!" said Smash. But Stone kept right on playing the Down Riff. As he played the Cave Boys gradually realized that what Stone said was true. Any riff that puts the accent on a Wailing Note or Note of Resolution will sound terrific when accompanying a blues or rock n' roll chord progression.

"You see, boys," the harp player finally said, "these riffs aren't exact. They're basic moves you can make on your harp. But *how* you make the move depends on the music you're accompanying, and what feels best to you."

"But how do you know what riff to play next?" asked Smash.

"Dig it," Stone replied. "Playing harp is like being in a good conversation. You don't know what you're going to say next; and if you tried to plan it, you'd probably get tongue-tied.

"You'll learn the language. Then you let what comes out of your mouth be a complete surprise. You catch on to the flow and feeling of the music and trust yourself.

"And if you make a mistake, say, playing 5 draw instead of 4 draw, don't worry about it. Just incorporate the 5 draw into the music.

80

Invent your own blues lick."

"How?" asked Krok.

"Lots of ways. But the most obvious is by sliding back to the 4 draw and wailing. The result would be:

Five Draw Mistake
3 ③ 4 ⑤ ④

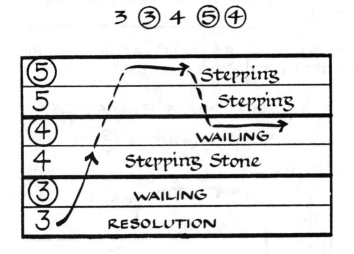

Stone played the 5 Draw Mistake.

"Hey, that's pretty good," said Smash. "I guess mistakes aren't really so bad after all."

"Not when you make them on purpose," winked Stone.

More Music on Holes Three and Four

"In case you haven't noticed," said Stone, "holes 3 and 4 are a veritable orchestra. There are so many patterns to play here that I couldn't begin to count them all.

"For instance, you can join the Up Riff and the Down Riff so they form one lick: the Up and Down Blues Riff."

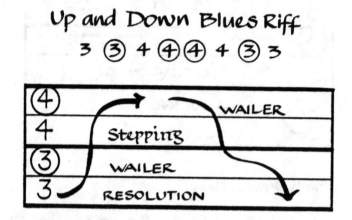

"The Up and Down Blues Riff starts out on Note of Resolution 3 blow. The 3 blow lets you know where home base is, where the music starts and ends. Then you take the Up Riff to the 4 draw Wailing Note. Play this 4 draw a long time to create tension.

"Then (and this is important), you pause. End of the Up Riff. Enter the Down Riff. Four draw, 4 blow, now a long moan of a 3 draw that creates tension...and FINALLY your Note of Resolution 3 blow.

"Now you guys try it."

It was hard work teaching these Neanderthals to play Cross Harp. But one thing about cave men, they were willing to work hard. Thus, in a couple of hours, all the Cave Boys (even Smash, who paid an extra 5 clams for a new harp) were sounding pretty good on the Up and Down Riff.

Gref threw another piece of wood on the fire. Smoke billowed through the cave and Stone gave him a dirty look. "Okay," he finally coughed, "I'm going to show you new licks and patterns on holes 3 and 4."

He squatted on the dirt floor of the cave and used a twig to draw some primitive diagrams.

"For instance, instead of playing 4 draw, 4 blow, 3 draw, 3 blow, play 4 draw, 4 blow, 3 draw, 4 *draw*. That's right. Instead of resolving tension, slide back to the 4 draw Wailer – and create tension."

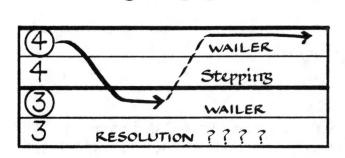

"You can play the 4 Draw Surprise over and over, and it will always fit in with the I-IV-V chord progression. Then, when you're tired of creating tension, finish your pattern with a 3 blow.

"And it sounds real good to alternate the 4 Draw Surprise with the Up Riff and the Down Riff. Like this..."

Stone put his harp to his mouth, puckered, and began to play in a clear, throbbing tone.

④ 4 ③ 3 (Down Riff)
④ 4 ③ ④ (4 Draw Surprise)
3 ③ 4 ④ (Up Riff)
④ 3 ③ 3 (Down Riff)

"Hey!" shouted Krok, "That sounds just like a little blues song!"

"Of course," said Stone. "That is because the first riff established home base, the next two riffs created tension, and the final riff returned to home base."

"And you did all that on two harmonica holes," said Smash. Thinking of the ton load of drums he had to carry around just to make a little music, he shook his head slowly.

"Maybe I've been playing the wrong instrument," he said.

"Careful," laughed Stone. "There's only one harp player in this band."

Two Draw

"Here's one of the best licks I know," said Stone. "I call it the Good Morning Riff because it sounds snappy and bright. It uses 2 draw as a Note of Resolution. Two draw is the same note as 3 blow. I find I use 2 draw when I'm playing a riff that comes from the bottom of the harp (such as the Good Morning Riff), and that I use the 3 blow Note of Resolution when I play a riff in the midrange of the harp (such as the Down Riff)."

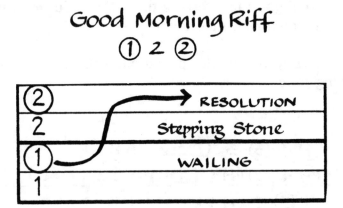

Stone played the Good Morning Riff a few times. Sure enough, it did sound snappy and bright. But when the Cave Boys tried, the riff sounded like it hadn't had a good night's sleep in weeks. The trouble was with the 2 draw. None of the beginning harp players could get a sound out of the rebellious note.

"What the heck's wrong with my 2 draw?" Smash asked. He peered angrily into the little square hole.

"The low draw notes give everyone trouble," Stone said. "The tendency is to tighten up when you suck on them. When they don't respond, the tendency is to suck even harder. Good way to break your harp.

"But if you want to play 2 draw right, try this. Take your harp out of your mouth. Now, rub your lips. Pinch them. Pucker up. Now relax...

"Consider, gentlemen, if you placed a straw up to that 2 draw and gently sucked, the note would play perfectly. But the way *you* go about playing the 2 draw Note of Resolution, forcing the air into your throat, you can't even get a sound. Hah!

"Put your harp back into your mouth, push it up towards your nose. Gently, very gently, draw a controlled stream of air to the roof of your mouth. *Coax* that note out. Keep the feeling light and airy. That note will come, but you gotta persuade it."

Armed with this new advice, the Cave Boys went to work on the 2 draw. Gref got it first – probably because he was a more relaxed type of guy. But before long, all the Cave Boys were playing the 2 draw, and the Good Morning Riff.

"Like any riff I show you," said Stone, "the Good Morning Riff can be played with many variations. Try tonguing the 2 draw in triplets. When you reach that Note of Resolution, give it three syllables as in **ta ta ta.**

$$① \ 2 \ ② \ \bullet \ \bullet$$

Or bounce back and forth between the 2 draw and 2 blow.

$$① \ 2 \ ② \ 2 \ ②$$

"You also can use the Good Morning Riff as a starting place for a pattern that takes you up to 3 draw."

Good Morning Three Draw
① 2 ② ③

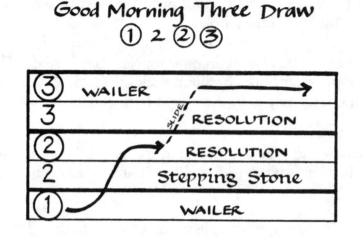

"Or, you can continue the riff up to 4 draw."

Good Morning Four Draw
① 2 ② ③ 4 ④

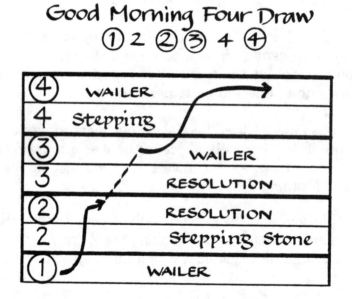

"But for simple accompaniment to a song you don't know that well, the Good Morning Riff ending on 2 draw: 1 draw, 2 blow, 2 draw — with a little tonguing action thrown in on the 2 draw is the safest way to go. Play it over and over, changing the timing and feeling to fit the music. It will never make a mistake."

86

Surprise Resolution

"If you've been paying attention," Stone said, "you've probably noticed that most of the Cross Harp riffs I've shown you are built around Notes of Resolution 3 blow or 2 draw.

"Can't we use the other notes?" asked Smash?

"Of course you can, "said Stone patiently. "In fact, I want to show you a couple of patterns that resolve on the 6 blow Note of Resolution. Six blow is the same note as 3 blow and 2 draw, but it's up an octave. (See page 16) You can toot along on 6 blow through an entire song and never make a mistake.

"The first riff we should try is the Surprise Resolution. It starts as though you were playing the Down Riff: 4 draw, 4 blow, 3 draw… but instead of resolving on 3 blow, slide the harp up to Note of Resolution 6 blow.

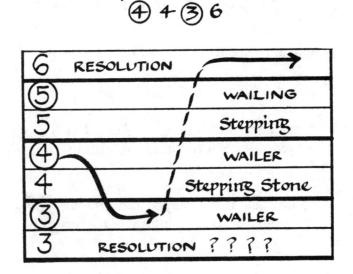

"Not bad," said Krok after he'd played the Surprise Resolution a few times. "It doesn't do what you'd expect, but it sounds good anyway. What else can you do with the 6 blow?"

"Why not go into the 6 draw?" suggested Gref. "I see here on your Cross Harp Map that it's a Wailing Note. Maybe I can create tension on the 6 draw and resolve it on the 6 blow."

Gref played a long cry on the 6 draw. Then, very gently, he brought it home to the Note of Resolution, 6 blow.

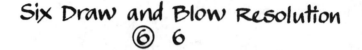

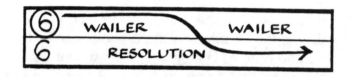

"That's really sweet," said Krok. "But here's an idea. Tongue the 6 draw to create even more tension."

The shaggy-haired guitarist put the harp in his mouth, puckered to get a clear single note, and drew on hole 6. Keeping one long draw, he tongued *ta ta taaaaaaa*.

Then, he stopped and looked at the rest of the Cave Boys with a sly smile.

"C'mon..." complained Smash.

"If you don't play that 6 blow, I will," said Gref.

Stone threw his head back and laughed. "Boy, that 6 draw sure created tension. I mean, it's still hanging there in the air. Somebody's got to resolve it."

"I can't stand it," Smash said. He played the 6 blow. There was a tremendous sense of release, of resolution, a feeling of being able to breathe again.

Krok looked at his harmonica in amazement. "Hey, this is a powerful little thing, isn't it?"

Good Old Six Blow

"Here's a nice little lick that will take you from Note of Resolution 6 blow down to Note of Resolution 3 blow or 2 draw," said Stone. "It's kind of like a scale."

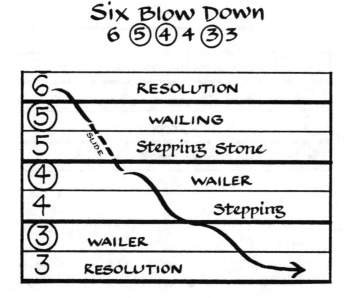

Tapping his foot 1 – 2 – 1 – 2 Stone played the 6 Blow Down a few times. "Now, one of the tricks in playing this lick is the way you move the harp from 5 draw to 4 draw. You SLIDE the harp, continuing to draw. If you do it by drawing on hole 5, stopping the draw, moving the harp to hole 4, and starting your draw again, the riff will sound clumsy."

"See what you mean," said Gref after he slowly played the 6 Blow Down. "What do you call that?"

"A DRAW SLIDE," said Stone. "It's one of those little details that can make a huge difference. And heck, it's not hard to keep drawing as you move the harp. Sure improves your music, though."

The Cave Boys played with the 6 Blow Down for several minutes, stomping out a 1 – 2 – 1 – 2 rhythm and putting the riff into this rhythmic framework.

After everyone had the hang of it, Stone said, "Now another thing you can do is stop the riff on 4 draw and create tension."

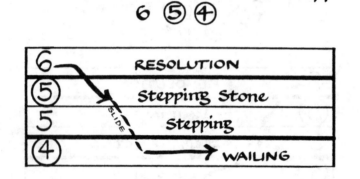

"You can play this pattern slowly, or fast, over and over, finally resolving the tension on a Note of Resolution using the Good Morning Riff, the Down Riff, the Surprise Resolution or any other sequence of notes that ends on the 2 draw, 3 blow, 6 blow, or 9 blow."

"So tell me," asked Gref, "when you play, do you think to yourself, 'Now I'm gonna play the Surprise Resolution. Now I'm gonna create tension on 6 draw?' Do you follow some kind of map?"

"I never do that," said Stone. "It would petrify me to play harp and think at the same time. No, playing harp is like dancing. You just blow and draw, warble and wail, and it comes out the way it's supposed to. And even if it isn't perfect, you still have a good time.

"And isn't that the whole point of playing music – to have a good time?"

"Then what's the purpose of learning all these riffs?" asked Smash. "Why not just pick the ol' harmonica up and play it?"

"I think you should," replied Stone. "When you practice, you should get your 1 – 2 – 1 – 2 beat going, try a few of the licks you've learned

90

from me, then leave those behind and play your own. After a few minutes of *not using* the stuff you've memorized, try the riffs again, always keeping your two stomp beat.

"By going back and forth between memorizing and being spontaneous, you'll be teaching yourself and having a good time. After a few days of working this way, the licks you've memorized will have become part of the way you pick the harp up and play it. They'll be natural. Know what I mean?"

Stone looked at his watch, a small Timex strapped to his wrist with dinosaur sinew. "Listen fellows, it's been hours. Haven't I earned my clams yet?"

"Is there more to the harmonica?" asked Krok.

"Well, of course," said Stone. "But it would take hours to cover everything: bending notes, using your hands, playing these riffs to a I-IV-V cycle, using microphones and amps. Don't you think you've heard enough? What about my clams?"

"What about the notes above 6 draw?" Krok persisted.

"Well, they're a little more difficult than the notes on holes 1 through 6; but if you want to know about them, I'll tell you."

"If you want your clams," said Smash, "you'll tell us."

Nine Blow

Stone squatted in the dirt of the cave. The fire reflected dual images on his aviator glasses.

"Okay," he began. "Holes 1 through 6 are the nuts and bolts of simple Cross Harp. Still, the holes above 6 will add drama to your harp playing.

"When learning these high notes, it's a good idea to practice on your lower harps: **G, A** flat or **A**. Since these harps are pitched a little lower, the high notes aren't nearly as difficult to play."

Stone took an **A** harp from his harmonica bag and played a 9 blow.

Nine Blow

```
┌─────────────────────────────────────────────┐
│  9 ───────────────────►  RESOLUTION          │
└─────────────────────────────────────────────┘
```

"Nine blow," he said, "is your Note of Resolution. It's the same note as 6 blow, only up an octave. It's the same note as 2 draw and 3 blow, but up two octaves." Stone gave **A** harps to Smash, Gref and Krok and let them work on the high, difficult 9 blow.

"Nine blow feels different than your lower notes," Stone said. "I change the shape of my lips and throat for this one. The airstream feels finely focused, and comes from my head rather than my throat or body as it does for the lower notes."

Nine blows (and pieces of 10 blows and 8 blows) screeched through the cave's musty air. "Takes a while to get the hang of this end of your harp," said Stone. "But it's worth it. There are some good licks up here."

"Such as?" asked Krok.

"Such as the 9 Blow Down," said Stone. "It takes you from the 9 blow Note of Resolution down to the 6 blow Note of Resolution.*

Stone cupped his hands around his harp and played a high, smooth lick starting on the 9 blow, lightly touching the 9 draw, the 8 blow, the 8 draw (creating a tiny bit of tension on this Wailing Note), sliding to the 7 draw, creating tension on the Wailing Note 6 draw and finally resolving on the 6 blow Note of Resolution.

"Remember," said Stone, "on holes 7 through 10, blow notes are higher than draw notes. Practicing 9 Blow Down will help you get a feeling for this. By the way, 9 Blow Down is the same riff as 6 Blow Down, but is up an octave.

92

Nine Blow Down
9 ⑨ 8 ⑧ ⑦ ⑥ 6

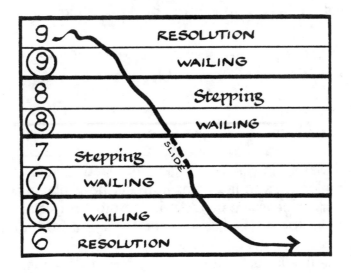

"Now, let me show you the 6 Blow Up. This is a Cross Harp lick that takes you from 6 blow to 9 blow.

Six Blow Up
6 ⑦⑧ 8 9

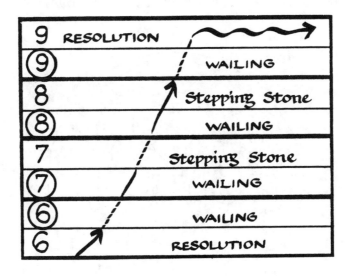

Each of the Cave Boys attempted to play the 6 Blow Up, but the riff was difficult and demanding (still is, as a matter of fact), especially getting a clean sound on the 9 blow and the 8 draw.

"How long did it take you to learn to play these high notes?" asked Gref.

"Man, I'm still learning," answered Stone. "Lots of times that 9 blow will just take off on me, or I'll try to play it and only get half the note. Sounds awful..."

"I've heard," said Krok.

Through his aviator glasses, Stone gave the lead guitarist a long, hard and dirty look. Even if he was a funky, harp-playing Cave Boy, Stone was a pretty sensitive guy. And, like most musicians, it was a lot easier for him to criticize himself than to hear it from others.

"Oh, yeah?" he finally said. He put his **A** harp to his lips. A long cry of a 9 blow rang out. Then the harp slid down over the notes, bending, twisting, shrieking, descending over the 9 draw, the 8 blow, the 8 draw, the 7 draw, the 6 draw, to the 6 blow, then performing a draw slide through the 5 draw, 4 draw, 3 draw, 2 draw, 1 draw- and back up through the 2 blow, 2 draw, 3 draw, and finally resolving on 2 draw.

"That, my friends, is the Complete Blues Scale Down."

94

Complete Blues Scale Down
9 ⑨ 8 ⑧⑦⑥ 6 ⑤④③②① 2 ②③②

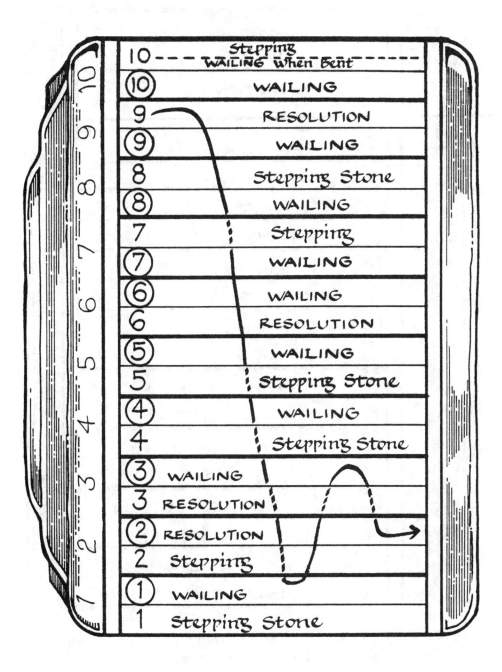

"And here," he said, "is the popular, amazing, and difficult-to-play Complete Blues Scale Up."

Complete Blues Scale Up
① 2 ② ③ 4 ④ 5 6 ⑦⑧ 8 9

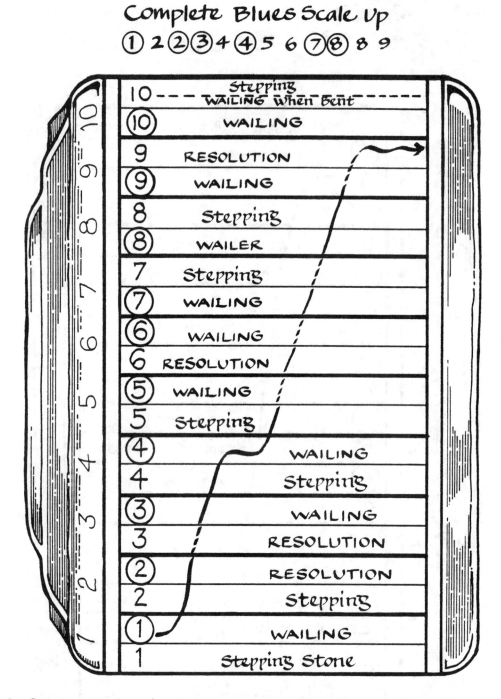

As Stone started on his 1 draw and moved swiftly and smoothly up the notes to 9 blow, Krok, Gref and Smash eyed each other. What was this guy trying to prove?

"Okay, Krok ol' boy," said Stone when the last echoes of the shrieking 9 blow had died. "It's your turn. Let's hear *you* play that lick."

96

"C'mon, man," said Krok. "I'm just starting out on harp. You know I can't play a lick like that."

"Don't have what it takes, eh?"

"Man, I play guitar..."

Stone laughed. "Not as difficult an instrument as harp, I guess."

"Listen, Stone..."

But Stone would not listen to Krok's excuses. Here he had spent hours showing these guys the secrets of Cross Harp, and Krok insults his playing.

"I'll bet you 20 clams you can't play this lick," Stone said.

Before Krok even had time to reply, Stone said, "I'll bet you *60* clams you can't play this lick."

Krok looked at the little harmonica resting in his hand. Its wooden edges and engraved hole numbers glistened in the firelight. He asked himself, could he play the Complete Blues Scale Up? Just once? Could he get lucky? Hmmmmmm 60 clams.

"Okay," he finally said. "You got a bet."

The Bet

Krok stood in the center of the cave. His face was streaked with sweat. His legs felt weak.

"Look," Gref said. "If you want to to chicken out, I'm sure Stone will..."

Krok hardly heard his worried bass player. He was deep inside himself, gathering his powers of concentration. Then, hands trembling, he cupped the boo boo reed beauty and put it to his puckered lips. Very softly, he played the 1 draw. A timid tone came from the harp. One draw. So far so good.

Knowing 1 draw was a Wailing Note, that he could play it as long as he wanted, Krok gently drew air through the reed inside the harp. (Since you know this same vital secret of Cross Harp, you might want to play your 1 draw as you read. It would give the story a nice musical backdrop.)

Now, from 1 draw, Krok would have to hop lightly to Stepping Stone 2 blow before he could find another safe spot. This would be Note of Resolution 2 draw.

①2②

He mentally rehearsed this small move of his harmonica and the draw-blow-draw transition required to get to the Note of Resolution. Okay, he finally said to himself, let's do it.

He moved the harmonica to hole 2. He blew and then he sucked. Two draw rang through. He made it. He was safe. For now.

As he drew on Note of Resolution 2 draw, he planned his next move. From the 2 draw, he'd have to go to 3 draw, continue on to hole 4, blow, and immediately draw — ending up, theoretically, on Wailing Note 4 draw. Another safe spot that would always work.

②③4④

Okay. He was going for it. Carefully, he slid the harp from the 2 draw to the 3 draw. Being a Wailing Note (usually used as a Stepping Stone in this lick), the 3 draw gave him time to think.

Yeah, the voice in his head told him, move the harp to hole 4 at the same time that you blow. Then draw. Yeah, Krok, you can do it. With a gentle pull he moved the harp to hole 4 as he blew and sucked. Perfect! He was playing the 4 draw. No one thought he'd make it to 2 draw and here he was, wailing on the 4 draw. He opened his eyes and looked across the firelit cave where Stone watched through flame-licked aviator glasses. What Krok would give to read his mind now.

Ta ta ta. He flicked his tongue on the fleshy ridge behind his teeth as he drew the 4 draw reed. *Ta ta ta.*

Might as well create a little tension while I'm here, he said to himself. *Ta ta ta.*

Nice touch, but this was no time for messing around. He had to think. (And if thinking is tough for 21st Century Man, consider what it must have been like for a Cave Boy.)

Now, this next move would not be as difficult. All he would have to do is move the harp to hole 5 and blow. Still blowing, he'd continue moving the harp to hole 6. And there he'd be – playing the 6 blow Note of Resolution.

④5 6

This is it, he thought. Gently he moved the harp to hole 5 and blew. Without breaking stride, he slid the harmonica to hole 6.

And there he was on 6 blow. *Ta ta ta.* His tongue tapped triumphantly on the moist ridge of his mouth just above his upper teeth. *Ta ta tatty ta taaaaah!*

What now?

Okay, he thought. First off, remember that the order of notes above 6 draw is reversed. From now on, blows are going to be higher than draws.

As for the move itself, it really didn't look that difficult. From the 6 blow Note of Resolution, slide the harp to hole 7 and draw. Continue sliding the harp to 8 draw.

6 ⑦ ⑧

Eight draw wasn't the most effective Wailing Note on the harp, but it would do for now. It would *have* to.

Bonzai, Cave Boy.

From the 6 blow, he sucked and moved the harp to hole 7 and to hole 8. Made it. But there was no time for congratulations. Eight draw just didn't sound that good as a Wailing Note.

But he was almost home. Almost 60 clams richer. All he'd have to do now was blow on hole 8 and blow on 9. Yeah. Go for it!

⑧ 8 9

So he did. He blew on the 8 and slid the harp to the 9. There he was – playing the 9 blow Note of Resolution. He had done it. He had actually played the Complete Blues Scale Up!

Still playing the 9 blow (wanting to savor the moment), Krok looked across the cave at Stone. To his surprise, the wirey harp player was smiling broadly. Hmmmmm, thought Krok, maybe Stone isn't such a bad guy after all.

"Yeah, man!" shouted Smash. He looked down at the tiny harmonica almost lost in his huge hand. If Krok could do it, so could he. The trick was to go real slow and to rest on the Wailing Note and Notes of Resolution.

"Right on," said Gref. He, too, was looking excitedly at his harmonica.

Ta ta ta! cried Krok's 9 blow. He made the note crow like a rooster, bark like a dog, wail like a fire engine. *Ta ta tatty ta taaaaah!* The triumphant 9 blow bounced and echoed off the cave walls. To all the Cave Boys, even Stone, the sound of this Note of Resolution was a thing of great beauty, a symbol of man's conquest over the unknown, a tribute to his ability to learn new skills.

Krok lowered the harp from his lips and smiled. Then he collapsed to the cave floor. Poor guy hadn't taken a decent breath in what seemed like hours.

<p style="text-align:center">~~~</p>

Notes

* There is no one way to play any of these riffs. The idea is to MOLD them to the music, to the beat, to your mood.

* When you make a mistake, DON'T STOP PLAYING. Simply continue blowing and drawing until you get to a Note of Resolution or a Wailing Note. When in doubt, fake it.

* When practicing these blues riffs, keep a steady 1 – 2 – 1 – 2 or 1 – 2 – 3 – 4 beat going with your foot.

* Use TONGUING to add rhythm and tension to Wailing Notes and Notes of Resolution.

* SIMPLICITY and REPETITION are important features of good harp music. For instance, the Good Morning Riff played again and again will usually sound better than the Complete Blues Scale Down or Complete Blues Scale Up.

* Feel free to use the patterns in this chapter as inspiration for making up your own blues patterns.

* Some of the riffs in this chapter are quite difficult. Don't feel you need to be able to play them before reading on.

SIX

Three Chords of the Blues: Playing Solo

Say good bye to that ancient cave where you learned your first blues riffs and pucker up to modern day harmonica music. Chapter VI gets you playing solo harp in I-IV-V blues cycles. Quite possibly this is the most important chapter in the book. Enjoy.

Solo Harp

There you are, playing your harmonica all by yourself, playing *solo*. You play the Up Riff. You play the Down Riff. You play the Blues Scale Down. You play the Good Morning Riff. The riffs you've been practicing sound great, but how do you link them together into one cohesive jam?

When you're playing with a guitar or a piano, there doesn't seem to be any problem. That's because these instruments play the chords and chord cycles. All the harp does is accompany.

But when you're playing by yourself, it's more difficult. The question you ask yourself is: which riff do I play now?

There are many approaches to playing solo harp music. You can play riffs to create and resolve tension. An example of this is playing the Up Riff (ending on Wailing Note 4 draw), pausing, and playing the Down Riff (resolving the tension on 3 blow).

You can play to create a rhythmic effect. You can do this by tonguing one note, say 3 blow, to a staccato train rhythm, using the Up Riff to wail on 4 draw, and returning to the rhythmic 3 blow.

You can also play your blues riffs in cycles – specifically I-IV-V cycles. When you play your solo music in a I-IV-V cycle, the I Chord of Resolution establishes home base. The IV Stepping Stone Chord moves the music away from home. The Dominant Wailer V Chord moves the music further still. Returning to the I Chord of Resolution provides a sense of completion of the cycle and can also signify the start of a new cycle.

Here's a simple I-IV-V chord cycle for Cross Harp. It's so short and easy you could call it a mini-cycle. Stomping out a 1 – 2 – 1 – 2 beat, play this cycle over and over. Give each chord two beats. Add tonguing to give special feeling. Imagine these sounds as a musical wheel and make that wheel roll.

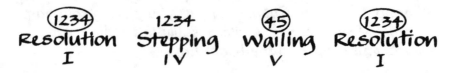

1234	1234	45	1234
Resolution	Stepping	Wailing	Resolution
I	IV	V	I

Single Note Cycles

Playing Cross Harp, the single notes that express the I Chord of Resolution are the Notes of Resolution 2 draw, 3 blow, 6 blow and 9 blow.

The notes that express the IV Stepping Stone Chord are Stepping Stone Notes 1 blow, 4 blow, 7 blow and 10 blow.

The single notes expressing the V Dominant Wailer Chord are Wailing Notes 1 draw, 4 draw and 8 draw. Three draw bent down and 6 draw will also work.

Giving each note two beats, play this I-IV-V single note mini-cycle.

Here's a mini-cycle that has you play the Wailing Note before you play the Stepping Stone Note.

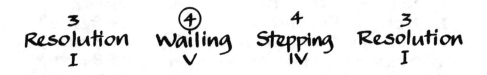

Try tonguing every note in this mini-cycle twice. Try tonguing in triplets. Tongue as though the harp were having a conversation with itself, making some sounds long and others short. No matter what your tonguing pattern, give each note two steady stomps of your foot. Make that harp go!

Single note progressions can also be played on the low end of your harp. Two draw is the same note as 3 blow. One blow is the same note as 4 blow, but an octave lower. Also one octave down, 1 draw is the same note as 4 draw.

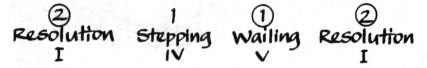

②   1   ①   ②
Resolution   Stepping   Wailing   Resolution
I   IV   V   I

Tonguing every note of the above progression will get your rhythm going. NOT tonguing the final 2 draw will produce a stronger feeling of resolution. Keep that foot, mouth and breath going as you play progression over and over.

Twelve Bars That Sound So Good

Anyone who listens to the blues has heard the 12 bar blues cycle. It's a long, slow progression with a steady 4 stomp beat. The term "12 bars" refers to 12 sections, each consisting of 4 beats. Playing clear single notes and stomping 1 – 2 – 3 – 4 – 1 – 2 – 3 – 4, play this single note blues cycle again and again. Tonguing each note will help make it more bluesy.

Twelve Bars for Beginners Cycle

I	Note of Resolution	3	(4 Beats)
IV	Stepping Stone Note	4	(4 Beats)
I	Note of Resolution	3	(4 Beats)
I	Note of Resolution	3	(4 Beats)
IV	Stepping Stone Note	4	(4 Beats)
IV	Stepping Stone Note	4	(4 Beats)
I	Note of Resolution	3	(4 Beats)
I	Note of Resolution	3	(4 Beats)
V	Dominant Wailer Note	④	(4 Beats)
IV	Stepping Stone Note	4	(4 Beats)
I	Note of Resolution	3	(4 Beats)
V	Dominant Wailer	④	(4 Beats)

(Start the cycle again)

106

Riff Cycles

The next stage in playing dynamite solo Cross Harp to the I-IV-V progression is to use riffs that:

1. End on a Note of Resolution to express the I chord.
2. End on Stepping Stone Note 1 blow, 4 blow, 7 blow or 10 blow to express the IV chord.
3. End on Wailing Note 1 draw, 4 draw, 6 draw, 8 draw or 3 draw bent down to express the V chord.

For instance, the Down Riff ends on 3 blow. Use it as a Riff of Resolution.

Down Riff

④ 4 ③ 3

To express the IV chord, play a riff that ends on a Stepping Stone Note, say, 4 blow.

Tongue the 4 draw three times, then play 4 blow.

To play a Dominant Wailer V Riff, use Wailing Note 4 draw in the Up Riff.

Up Riff

3 ③ 4 ④

Resolve your blues cycle with the Down Riff, giving the home base 3 blow a feeling of finality and completion.

Down Riff

④ 4 ③ 3

Try playing these riffs so they create a blues cycle.

Beginner's Blues Cycle

I	Riff of Resolution	④ 4 ③ 3
IV	Stepping Stone Riff	④④④ 4
V	Dominant Wailer Riff	3 ③ 4 ④
I	Riff of Resolution	④ 4 ③ 3

You can play the Wailing V Riff BEFORE you play the Stepping Stone IV Riff and get another simple blues progression.

Stomp N' Tongue Blues Cycle

I	Riff of Resolution	④ 4 ③ 3
V	Dominant Wailer Riff	3 ③ 4 ④
IV	Stepping Stone Riff	④④④ 4
I	Riff of Resolution	④ 4 ③ 3

On the low end of your harp, use 2 draw to end your Riff of Resolution, 1 blow as a Stepping Stone Riff ending, and 4 draw to put the wail in your Wailing Riff.

Good Morning Blues Cycle

I	Riff of Resolution	① 2 ②②
IV	Stepping Stone Riff	2 3 2 1
V	Dominant Wailer Riff	④ 4 ③④
I	Riff of Resolution	④ 4 ③ 3

Another way to play the I-IV-V cycle is to use 6 blow to end your Riff of Resolution and 6 draw to create the Dominant Wailer Riff.

Blues for Pamina Cycle

I	Riff of Resolution	⑥ 6 ⑤④ 4 ③ 3
IV	Stepping Stone Riff	④④④ 4
V	Dominant Wailer Riff	④⑤ 6 ⑥
I	Riff of Resolution	⑥⑥⑥ 6

108

More Solo Cycles

Here are some blues cycles that use more than four riffs. Pause between riffs if you want, but keep the beat going.

Prosperity Blues Cycle

I	Riff of Resolution	3 ③ 4 ④ ④ 4 ③ 3
IV	Stepping Stone Riff	④④④ 4
I	Riff of Resolution	④ 4 ③ 3
V	Dominant Wailer	④④④④
IV	Stepping Stone Riff	④④④ 4
I	Riff of Resolution	④ 4 ③ 3
V	Dominant Wailer	3 ③ 4 ④
	or	
I	Riff of Resolution	3 ③③ 3

This blues cycle can be concluded by playing the Riff of Resolution twice. Or, it can be continued by playing the Riff of Resolution once and then playing a Wailing Riff. Playing this Wailing Riff at the end of the blues cycle is called a TURN-AROUND. The turn-around ends the blues cycle in a state of tension on the V chord, and makes you want to play it again.

The first two times you play the above cycle, use the turn-around. The third time you play it, resolve on the Riff of Resolution.

When you're able to bend the 2 draw, 3 draw, or 4 draw and 6 draw, be sure to work them into these riffs.

This next blues cycle uses another combination of Wailing Notes and Notes of Resolution.

Jamaica Blues Cycle

I   Riff of Resolution   ⑥⑥⑥ 6
V   Dominant Wailer   6 ⑤④④
IV Stepping Stone Riff   ④⑤④ 4
I   Riff of Resolution   ① 2 ②②
V   Dominant Wailer   3 ③ 4 ④
IV Stepping Stone Riff   ④④④ 4
I   Riff of Resolution   ① 2 ②②

V   Dominant Wailer   ②③ 4 ④
            or
I   Riff of Resolution   3 ③③ 3

This example of a blues cycle uses the high end of your harp. Up here, 9 blow is often used as a Note of Resolution. Eight draw is a Wailing Note, and 7 blow is a Stepping Stone Note.

Tia's Blues Cycle

I   Riff of Resolution   ⑧⑨ 9 9
V   Dominant Wailer   9 ⑨ 8⑧
IV Stepping Stone Riff   ⑧⑧⑧ 7
I   Riff of Resolution   ⑥⑥⑥ 6
V   Dominant Wailer   6 ⑦ 7 ⑧
IV Stepping Stone Riff   ⑧ 9 ⑨ 7
I   Riff of Resolution   ⑥⑥⑥ 6

V   Dominant Wailer   6 ⑦ 7 ⑧
            or
I   Riff of Resolution   6 ⑦⑧⑦ 6

Muddy's Blues Cycle

You will recognize this classic blues cycle as soon as you play the first riff. Rythm is important here. Count 1-2-3-4. Play each riff on the 1-2 and pause, shout, breathe or grunt on the 3-4.

I   3   4   ③ ②   "Oh, yeah!"

I   3   4   ③ ②   "That's it!"

I   3   4   ③ ②   "You got it!"

I   3   4   ③ ②   "Alright!"

IV   ② ③ ② ③   4   "That's it!"

IV   ② ③ ② ③   4   "Can't help it!"

I   3   ④ ③ ②   "Scratch my back!"

I   3   ④ ③ ②   "Scratch your back!"

V   ④ ⑤ ④ ⑤ ④   "I love it!"

IV   ④ ④ ③ ④   4   "I want it!"

I   3   4   ③ ②   "You got it!"

V   ④   4   ③ ④   4   ③ ④   "Come on, now!"

Tilting the back of the harp up puts it back further in your lips. This can really improve your tone.

Hootchie Kootchie Blues Cycle

Here's a famous riff typically played by harp masters doing the Muddy Waters thing. If you're not familiar with Muddy Waters, you have a pleasurable education ahead. You will find this blues cycle played on the low end of your harp on page 130.

I   ④ ⑤ ④ ⑤ 6   **"That's good!"**

I   ④ ⑤ ④ ⑤ 6   **"That's bad!"**

I   ④ ⑤ ④ ⑤ 6   **"You're so cool!"**

I   ④ ⑤ ④ ⑤ 6   **"Don't get cocky!"**

IV   6 ⑦ 6 ⑦ 7   **"Got milk?"**

IV   6 ⑦ 6 ⑦ 7   **"Kiss me!"**

I   ④ ⑤ ④ ⑤ 6   **"Don't kiss me!"**

I   ④ ⑤ ④ ⑤ 6   **"So good!"**

V   ⑧ ⑨ ⑧ ⑨ ⑧   **"So fine!"**

IV   ⑧ ⑧ ⑦ ⑧ 7   **"I need you!"**

I   ④ ⑤ ④ ⑤ 6   **"Blow, baby!"**

V   6 6 ⑤ ④ ④   **"Do it again!"**

112

Notes

* The framework of folk, blues, rock, country western, reggae, etc. is the I-IV-V progression.

* When playing with a band, let the bass and guitar express the I-IV and V, while you use harmonizing notes to fill in and take leads.

* When playing solo, the harp player can play riffs that completely express the progression.

* The basic idea is to play riffs that end on a Note of Resolution to express the I chord, riffs that end on a Wailing Note to express the V chord, and riffs that end on Stepping Stone Note 1 blow, 4 blow, 7 blow or 10 blow to express the IV chord.

* The I-IV-V blues cycle is NOT CARVED IN CONCRETE. The order of riffs can be changed and one riff can be substituted for another.

* The only set rule is that the harp player establishes a home base.

* As the harp player plays the cycle, he or she can use 3 blow as a Note of Resolution one time, 6 blow or 9 blow the next time. Similarly, one Wailing Note can be exchanged for another, one Stepping Stone for another.

* Learning the progressions in this chapter will enhance your harp playing; but the way they sound, the tempo at which they're played, their overall feeling is up to you.

SEVEN

Falling in Love With Bending

Okay, Okay. It's a sappy illustration, but how else can you best describe the feeling you have the very first time you bend a note? This chapter takes you from beginning to advanced on a variety of bending and other tone-altering techniques. Be patient with the hard stuff and keep reading because the book gets easier.

Let's Learn to Bend

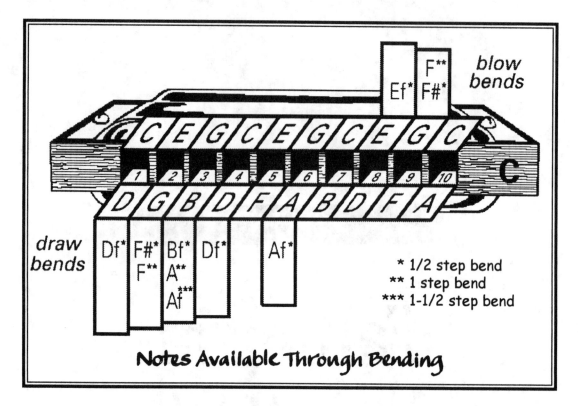

Notes Available Through Bending

But old Stoney didn't tell Krok and the boys everything that day in the jam cave. For instance, he didn't tell them that he was going to make them a big clam dinner that very night. He didn't tell them about the chick singer he had fallen in love with. He also withheld the secret arts of bending. So here they are. But, please beware: **no one who reads these pages will ever play harmonica the same again.**

Bending is the art of lowering and raising the pitch of a harmonica note by changing the direction of the air column as it enters or leaves your lips for draw or blow bends. For instance, 4 draw can be sucked down to 4 draw bent. On your **C** harp, this is going from **D** to **D** flat. The chart above shows the most commonly used bends.

To bend, draw in a compressed column of pressurized air.

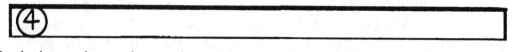

Suck that column down, down, down and hopefully, the note will follow.

116

How Bending Works

blow

Take a closer look at your harmonica. The sound is created by your wind vibrating a thin strip of metal called a "reed," set inside a "reed-plate." The longer the reed, the lower the tone. The harmonica has two reed-plates, each with ten reeds. The plate on top responds to blows. The reed-plate on the bottom responds to draws.

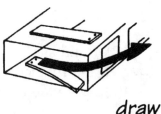

draw

What happens when you bend 4 draw? If you curve the air in your mouth just right, so the 4 draw reed vibration moves across the reed in just the right way, the 4 blow will begin to vibrate sympathetically, and this vibration will slow down the 4 draw. Slowing down the vibration lowers the pitch of the note.

This was only discovered recently.

To Stone, it was more of a magical, mystical, spiritual thing that he did with his mind, breath and body and deeply involved his throat, lips, and tongue. And his nose. Let's not forget Stone's honker.

Close Nose to Bend

When Stoney thought about his nose, what he really meant was his whole sinus system. Opening the nose helps you play notes unbent. Closing your nose helps you bend them. (And both bent and unbent notes are important.)

To close your nose off, **sniff** as you draw 4 and let the natural suction close off your nostrils. This might feel a little like wrinkling your nose. This nasal-closing changes the back pressure in such a way that a bend is almost inevitable. To bring the pitch up, open the nostrils.

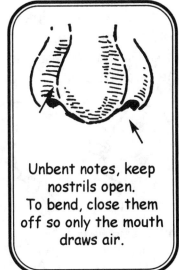

Unbent notes, keep nostrils open. To bend, close them off so only the mouth draws air.

117

Use Vowel Sounds to Bend
Eeeeerrrrrrrr

A few thousand years after Stone and the boys made history, master harp player and session man Stanley Behrens of Venice, California, discovered the magic vowel sound that opens up the back of the throat in just the right way to receive the airstream.

Give this a try by thinking "wee" on your 4 draw. As you close your nose, change your throat to an "rr" (as in her) position and suck the airstream to that position. Maintaining back pressure, return to "ee" and suck the note back up.

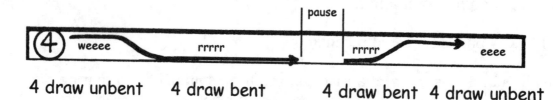

4 draw unbent   4 draw bent   4 draw bent   4 draw unbent

Displacement of Back Pressure

Another way of thinking about bending: Take that compression, that cold airball of pressured airstream, and move it from the top of your throat to the bottom of your throat. This may involve opening up the bottom of your throat in the same way as when you say "er."

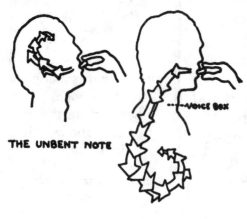

THE UNBENT NOTE

THE BENT NOTE

But saying "er" by itself won't do it. You have to actively, from your guts, suck that back pressure down the shaft of your throat and hold it.

Use your trembling stomach to hold the bend. To release the bend, bring the back pressure up to the top of your throat into your head.

Unbent notes are as important as bent notes. Learn both.

118

First Bend

Bending ain't easy. You knock your head against the wall for three weeks, a month, three months, three years...with no results, and then suddenly, somewhere, when you least expect it, that bend pops out. Congratulations! Now what?

Do it again. Do it again and again. Try to isolate what it is that you're doing so you remember it. Is it that new way you're relaxing your jaw? Is it because you suddenly understand what it means to suck the airstream down? Is it because you finally ignored these instructions? Whatever it is, as you bend again and again, try to identify something you can remember and use later.

Let's assume it's a 4 draw you're working on. Start at the top of the bend (4 draw unbent). Then bend your note (4 draw bent).

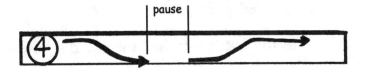

Pause. Stomp your foot. Grunt. You can even take the harp out of your mouth if you're in a particularly casual mood. Now, start where you left off–with the 4 draw bent down, and unbend it. This down-to-up, bent-to-unbent is an essential bending maneuver.

Using your tapping tongue, try these bends as well.

Tongue Bend

Tongue Wailer Bend

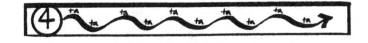

119

What Happens to a Riff or a Song When I Bend 4 Draw?

When you play 2nd position, 4 draw unbent (the **D** note) is the all-important 5th note of the **G** scale. It's

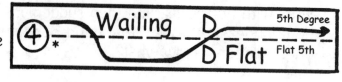

a Wailing Note that creates tension and can be adapted to play through an entire I-IV-V chord progression without making a mistake. (However, unless you bend it just a little, your harping won't sound bluesy.)

If you continue bending the 4 draw down, you will come to the **D** flat note, the flatted 5th. The flatted 5th is an essential note of the blues scale. Simply bending from from bent to unbent, bent to unbent is a blues solo unto itself. Try this:

Add the 4 draw bent to the Up Riff to feel this bend's power.

There are times in blues and jazz when the 4 draw bent is a target note. But most of the time, the 4 draw bent will clash unless connected to a 4 draw unbent.

Add the 4 draw bent to the Cross Harp Scale.

Go back to finger snapping, or some other form of setting a beat. Recall how snapping your fingers twice on each beat gave you 8th notes. Instead of snapping those digits twice, play two notes: 4 draw bent to unbent on each beat.

Four Notes in 3 Draw

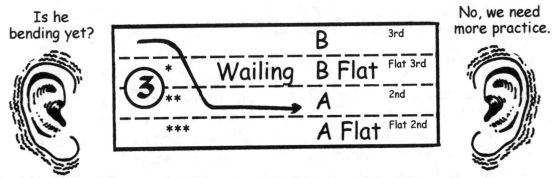

Is he
bending yet?

No, we need
more practice.

Behold the miracle! The 3 draw reed contains upon its tiny metal surface what a piano requires four piano keys to achieve.

Yet as Stone and every other harp man after him discovered, it is not always easy to harness the power. The pathway to harmonica excellence is strewn with misplayed 3 draw bends.

For some beginners the first challenge might be just making the note sound out. If the nose is closed, if air compression is pointed too far down in the body, if the lips are too tight, or if your jaw, throat, sinus or cheeks are clamped up, the only result you might achieve is a forlorn squeaky foghorn, a phenomenon called the **prebend**.

The most important things to know about bending can be found in instruction on single notes. The harp must be deep in your mouth. There must be strong, steady compression. Your face must be relaxed. You can't be out of breath. Instead, your entire mouth is sculpted for power. Your actual breath is small but powerful because of the way it's resisted at your lips and compressed throughout your body. Your embouchure, the cavity that accepts the harp, must be large and yet create a narrow airstream.

The 3 draw unbent starts with the nose open, the air pressure at the top of the throat, the mouth and throat cavities in an "ee" position. The 3 draw bends as the nose closes, the air pressure goes down the shaft, and the throat opens in a way similar to make the "rr."

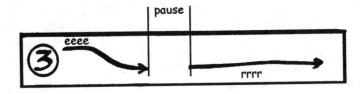

121

The Prebend Problem on 2 Draw and 3 Draw

As I mentioned, a **prebend** is 2 and 3 draw's half bent, uncontrolled fog horn that threatens to turn into a duck's squeal at any moment. There's a strong resistance, as though that reed doesn't want to be played. This phenomenon is called a prebend because in a sense, you are bending the reed, just a little bit incorrectly. The trick now is to learn to play the reed unbent. Then, you can start bending. This time, correctly.

One exercise that can quickly help you get over the prebend requires a very meditative frame of mind. The idea is to pretend that the only way you can breathe is through the 3 draw chamber of your harmonica.

Start with a single note on 3 draw or 2 draw that you softly draw and blow, and make each breath last about 10 seconds. Remember, you are not trying to bend, rather *unbend*. You will find yourself getting very focused, minimizing your breathing needs and shaping your mouth for optimum breath control.

As you struggle to survive, there are steps you can take to unbend your prebend.

TIPS ON UNBENDING 3d

1. Open up your nostrils so a teeny bit of air comes through.

2. Push the harp up toward your nose.
   Tilt the harp up toward your nose.

3. Relax your entire single note embouchure.

4. Move back pressure to the top of your throat and into your head and nasal passages.

5. Cut your volume of air in half.

122

Using the 3 Draw Bends

Bending to the right note is like singing, you need to hear and adjust. You may think that in order to hit the deepest of the bends, you need to bend deeper and deeper. The opposite is true: what you do is bend less and less. Let's start with no bend, then move progressively deeper.

The 3 Draw Unbent

In 2nd position, the unbent 3 draw is important in making major key music. Learn to play it as high as possible in your head and nose. When playing minor key music, the 3 draw unbent will almost always clash, so use the 3 draw*.

The 3 Draw Half Step Bend*

The tiniest 3 draw bend is the 3 draw*. On your **C** harp, it's a **B** flat, the flatted 3rd. When playing minor keys, you must play this note instead of 3 draw unbent. This small bend occurs naturally just from drawing. Use it in the blues scale, or in the Up Riff as you pass from one note to the next.

The 3 Draw Whole Step Bend**

If you bend a little bit more, you play an **A** note. I call this the middle bend. The **A** note is the 9th scale degree–an important note in blues and jazz. The 3 draw** **A** note also enjoys a special relationship with the **C** chord and is where we often go to get through the IV section of the I-IV-V chord progression. In 2nd position, the 3 draw** goes with major and minor key music.

The 3 Draw Step and a Half Bend***

The full-on 3 draw bend is the **A** flat, not used very much in 2nd position, at least by me. If, in the course of riffing, your 3 draw bent is always unpleasant, it may be because you are bending the 3 draw into **A** flat range.

GUITAR TUNER TIPS

A guitar tuner is a useful tool to see how accurately you're bending. Another gauge is to listen closely for bad notes. Often harp players play the **A** flat and the **A** when they should be on the **B** flat.

Bending Two Draw

As a rule of thumb (or lip), if you are able to get a clear single note on the 2 draw of your **C** harp, you are playing single notes correctly.

On the other hand, if your 2 draw won't respond, your single note technique needs help. Try moving the harp UP toward your nose. Relax your lips, but keep a deep, sensuous pucker. As you draw, direct that airstream to the roof of your mouth. Pull that note UP.

The unbent 2 draw is a Note of Resolution. It's the same note as 3 blow. The advantage of 2 draw is that you can get there quickly from 1 draw and 2 blow–and you can bend 2 draw down an entire step to the important blues note, the flatted 7th.

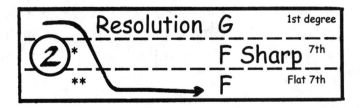

Start by getting a clear single note on 2 draw. Then, with a little sniff, suck the note down, deep into your voice box. Your 2 draw may distort, but that's okay as long as the note is actually lowering. In fact, a distorted bent 2 draw is one of the hallmark sounds of blues harp.

When the note pulls down, hold it there. Then gradually, opening your nose, allow the bent 2 draw to return to its unbent position.

Two Step Bend

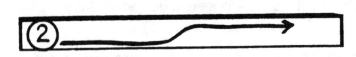

When you are able to bend 2 draw down and back up, try *starting* the bend with the bent 2 draw and slowly bring it up.

2 Draw Bent to 2 Draw Unbent

On the **C** harp, the 2 draw** is an **F**, the flatted 7th of the **G** scale, an essential blues note. The flatted 7th leads naturally to the Note of Resolution. In fact, in a crazy, off-kilter blues way, it can substitute for the Note of Resolution.

Since the blues is usually played in chords that use the flatted 7th note, a warbling 2 draw** can make a perfect slow blues accompaniment.

Articulate the bent 2 draw with a ta ta tonguing action as you slowly bring the note up.

Another way to use the 2 draw bent is to substitute it for the 2 draw unbent. Play the same riff twice. First time resolve on the 2 draw**. Second time on 2 draw.

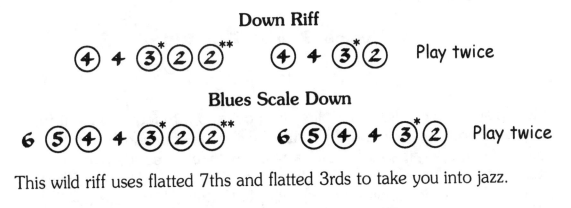

This wild riff uses flatted 7ths and flatted 3rds to take you into jazz.

Funky Five Draw Flatted 7th

When you play 2nd position, 5 draw is what I call a blues steppingstone. When it does harmonize, it does so in a slightly off-kilter way. Just sliding from 4 draw to 5 draw back to 4 draw gives you an idea of what this blues note can do. This **headshake** is very effective– particularly if you bend and unbend the 4 draw as you slide the harp.

means slide
back & forth

The 5 Draw Descender is a useful riff. Although it's 2nd position, it's a melodic line. Give it a try:

$$\text{(5)} \quad 5 \quad \text{(4)} \quad 5 \quad \text{(4)} \quad 4 \quad \text{(3)} \quad 3$$

The 5 draw is an **F** note on your **C** harp, the same note as 2 draw**, only up an octave.

This famous John Lennon riff uses the 5 draw to great effect.

"Love Me Do" Type Riff

$$\text{(5)} \quad 5 \quad \text{(4)} \quad 3 \quad \bullet \quad \text{(repeat)}$$

A popular song about a red-bellied bird that rocks can be played starting off on the 5 draw.

"Rockin' Robin" Type Riff

$$\text{(5)} \quad \bullet \quad 5 \quad \bullet \quad \text{(4)} \quad 5 \quad \text{(5)} \quad 5 \quad \text{(4)}$$

Over-playing the 5 draw in a blues improvisation, trying to bend it the way you would wail on a 4 draw, usually sounds amateurish. On the other hand, using it so it fits into a blues melody, or so it's part of a headshake makes a fine sound. Bluesy songs and chord progressions that use flatted 7th chords are more likely to find a home for the 5 draw than more melodic songs.

> To sound more melodic,
> use 5 blow as a stepping stone.
> To sound bluesy, add the 5 draw.

Six Draw Unbent and Bent

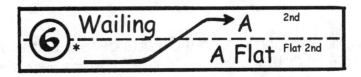

Six draw is the same note as the bent 3 draw, except it is an octave higher. You can tongue and bend it through an entire blues cycle. You can easily resolve the tension created by 6 draw by playing Note of Resolution 6 blow.

Six Draw Wail and Six Blow Resolution

Some effective bends on the 6 draw are:

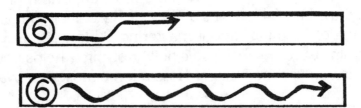

A riff that demonstrates the power of this easy bend is the Bent 6 Draw Down. The bent 6 draw sets up the unbent 6 draw to create a funky and compelling beginning to this familiar riff.

Bent 6 Draw Down

The High End–Cross Over at 6d & 7d

Above 6 draw, ol' harpoon's like a different boy. Starting at 7 draw, the draw notes are LOWER than the blows. To cross over and back from the high end to the low end, play two draw notes in a row as you move from the sixth hole to the seventh. Practicing scales like the ones below will help you adjust automatically.

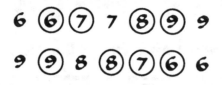

Bending 9 Blow

In most 2nd position playing, 9 blow is the most important of the high notes. Like 2 draw and 6 blow, it's a Note of Resolution–on your **C** harp a **G**. One of the great things about mastering 9 blow is that you can bend it down almost to an **F**. This flexibility of pitch helps you create tension and lets you use the Note of Resolution almost as a Wailing Note.

The first step in bending 9 blow is getting a clear single note. Then push the focused and compressed airstream forward and down into the harmonica. Closing your nose helps the bend. It is essential to have the support of your diaphragm, even though you're not using that much air.

To bring the bend up, let the focus of air pressure in the harmonica and your sinus' rise, and open your nostrils. For beginners and their loved ones, this is easiest on lower pitched harps such as **G** or **A**. A great place to finish a 2nd position solo is on the high 9 blow, bending it down to create tension, and then bringing it back up. You might achieve this kind of ending by substituting the 9 blow for a 2 draw, or 6 blow.

128

9 Blow Surprise

④ ← ③* 9

It is here a harp player might embellish the Note of Resolution with a long curve of sound downward and back up.

You might also get up to the 9 blow by taking a riff from the 6 blow.

6 ⑦ ⑧ 8 9

The only 2nd position do-re-mi scale on the harp goes from 6 blow to 9 blow. This is not a blues scale, rather a melodic one.

Cross Harp Diatonic Scale

6 ⑥ ⑦ 7 ⑧ 8 9* 9
do   re   mi   fa   so   la   ti   do

Jimmy Reed was a great blues player who specialized in songwriting, singing and high note harp solos. Defying conventional blues wisdom, he played many of these solos in 1st position Straight Harp–where the high Note of Resolution is the 7 blow and 9 blow is a Wailing Note. Check out the Straight Harp Up and Down Blues Riff.

Straight Harp Up and Down Blues Riff

7   8   ⑨   9*   9   pause   9*   9   ⑨   8   7

Perfecting 2 and 3 Draw Bends

The best practice scale that I know is actually for playing Straight Harp. However, it requires that you bend the 2 draw and 3 draw to their perfect pitches. Because it's such an elementary part of music, you can hear the notes you are bending to before you've actually played them. The scale is:

1   ①   2   ②**   ②   ③**   ③   4
do   re   mi   fa   so   la   ti   do

129

Blues Riffs, Cycles and Scales Using Bends

The riffs below are arranged in a blues cycle. They are also important riffs in their own right. You can repeat the riffs, break them out of the blues cycle presentation, build them into something original.

Up Riff I chord to V chord ②** ② ③* 4 ④* ④

Down Riff   V to VII chord ④* ④ 4 ③* ② ②**

Wailing Riff   V chord ④* ④ ⑤ ④ ⑤ ④* ④

Up and Down   I to IV to I ②** ② ③** 4 ③* ② ②*

Good Morning   V to II ① 2 ② ③**

Up Riff   V to IV ② ③* 4 ④* ④ 4

Good Morning   V to I ① 2 ② ③* 4 ③* ②

Turn Around   VII to V ②** ①

Hootchie Kootchie Cycle

I   ① ②** ① ②** ②   (Play 4 times)

IV   ② ③* ② ③* 4   (Play twice)

I   ① ②** ① ②** ②   (Play twice)

V   ④ ⑤ ④ ⑤ ④   (Play once)

IV   ④ ③* ④ 4   (Play once)

I   ① ②** ① ②** ②   (Play once)

V   ④ ⑤ ④ ⑤ ④   (Play once and start cycle again)

130

LITTLE WALTER RIFF

I took this from an old Little Walter version of "Rollin' and a Tumblin'." Play it fast, again and again.

②③②② ②③②

SUPER VII RHYTHM RIFF

This is the kind of riff that creates its own hook and can set the basis of a song. Even though it ends on the 2 draw bend, the flatted 7th, it expresses the I chord.

③* ②②** ② ③* ②②** (repeat riff)

BROOM DUSTER RIFF

This famous blues riff begins with a 6 blow or 3-6 blow tongue-block played in three groups of triplets.

6 ta ta ta   ta ta ta   ta ta ta taa   3 ③*②

6 ta ta ta   ta ta ta   ta ta taa

6 • ⑤ • ④ ← ③*

② • ③ • ② • 2 ①   Play twice...then repeat first line

STOP AND START SCALES ON DIFFERENT NOTES

Bluesify the second position no-bend scale by adding bent notes.

②** ② ③** ③ 4 ④* ④ ⑤ 6 ⑥* ⑥ 7 ⑧ 8 ⑨ 9

Change the meaning and direction of the scale by starting on different notes. For instance, start the scale on 3 draw, or 3 draw**. Start it on 2 draw** (as I did above), or even 2 blow.

Where you start the scale determines the riff's melodic direction. Where you end determines the chord you end up expressing.

Your music will get jazzier and jazzier.

131

Handcup Compression for Enriched, Swelling Tone

Think of your sound as subtle water in a stream and cup your hands around the harp airtight to hold the water. Now, when you play a single note, the inside of your palms will tickle from the compression of your breath. Curve out your hands and make your fingers flaccid so they join together. Those of you with sore hands are gripping too tightly. (Those of you with sore lips have the same malady!)

Cupping your hands around the harmonica with an airtight seal darkens and mellows the sound. Releasing the compressed tone within the cup by swinging open a finger or loosening a hand opens the tone, makes the tone louder and brasher, probably thinner, too. Doing this a couple of times gives you a wa wa effect.

The pictures on these pages show different approaches to cupping your harp. It is impossible to get an airtight seal if your hands are not relaxed.

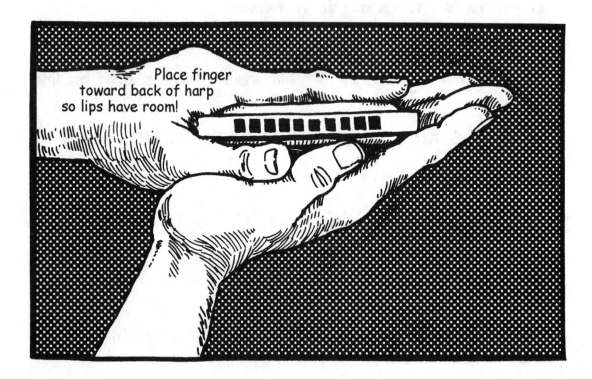

Place finger toward back of harp so lips have room!

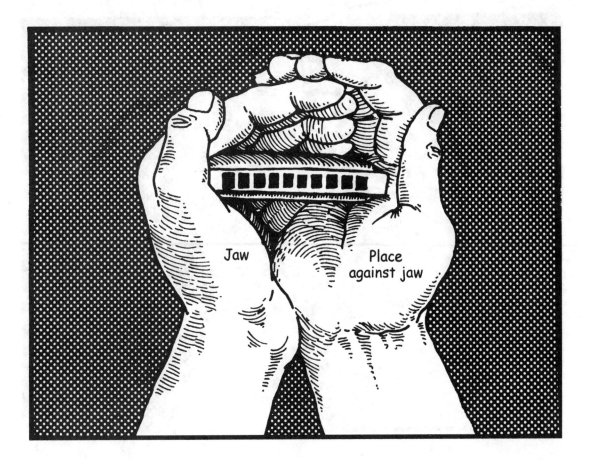

Depending on how you change your cup, going from closed to open, or opened to closed, or just keeping the middle ground of almost-airtight, you'll create effect after effect–another dimension to how your harp speaks the blues.

Earlier I talked about the concept of compression. The entire body–lips, throat, stomach–is sculpted to intensify the power of your breath. If you play with compression, you should be able to feel and further manipulate this compression with your hands.

The hand effects work best on holes 1 through 6. So allow your best cupping effect to be located on the lower end of the harp. Then just make adjustments when you move to the top end.

Notice how the thumb covers the higher holes on the illustration on page 134. Holding your thumb in this place helps make your cup airtight, and you can easily move your thumb out of the way when you play the high notes.

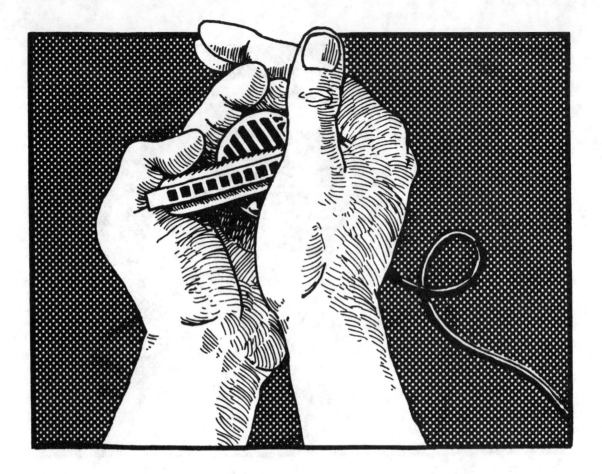

Playing with a microphone is a little different because now the hands are connecting the body and the harp to the mic. The effect of this airtight system is that you are practically putting the mic inside your mouth. Your cupped hands compress the harp's sound into the mic, and the mic compresses the sound into a wire plugged into an amp, which compresses it further. By compressed, I mean controlled, channeled, narrowed into an electronic richness.

The Astatic microphone shown here is a favorite for harp because of raunchy, yet potentially warm tone. I say "potentially" because it is not an easy mic to use–and the difficulty is indeed in cupping it and getting that airtight seal.

Your hands must be relaxed in the same way that they are when there is no microphone. Bring your hands together as though you were cupping water out of a stream. Allow your palms to relax into a concave bowl and make the microphone the deepest part of the bowl.

Remember, no matter how you amplify, or *whether* you amplify, it's all about TONE.

134

Notes

* The most important skill in harp playing is being able to get a clear, rich SINGLE note.

* To keep from running out of breath when playing harp, learn the trick of the SLOW INHALE.

* BENDING is a technique in which the harp player lowers the note by manipulating the airstream, pulling it DOWN into the lungs.

* Bending is very difficult if you don't have a good single note with an up and out pucker of your lips. It's not difficult when your single note technique is correct.

* Bending helps the harp player create tension. Below hole 6, bend 1 draw, 2 draw, 3 draw, 4 draw and 6 draw. Above hole 6, bend 8 draw, 9 blow and 10 blow.

* Bending can be combined with TONGUING.

* CUPPING your hands around the harp mellows tone and makes the harp say *oooooooo*. Opening your hands makes the harp say *ahhhhhhhh*.

* Use the instructions on hands to find the way of cupping the harp that feels best to you. Everybody's hands are different, and each harp player's cup is a little different.

Straight Harp Accompaniment

Straight Harp, or 1st Position, is the style of harmonica that often sounds best with ballads and folk-based rock. More melodic than Cross Harp, it's also easier to play. In Chapter Eight, Stone plays Straight Harp, brings a woman vocalist to practice, and the band tunes up.

The Mysterious Visitor

One Sunday afternoon Stone showed up for practice in a suit and tie.

"Hey!" demanded Smash. "What's going on here?"

Before Stone could answer, a woman stepped into the entrance of the cave. She was tall, slender, and most important to the chauvinist Cave Boys, good-looking.

"Guys," said Stone, "I'd like you to meet a friend of mine. This is Umm."

Six Cave Boy eyes went from Stone to Umm and back to Stone. True, Umm was a dish. But what was this "friend" stuff? If you wanted a woman, you grabbed her by the hair and dragged her back to the cave. You didn't call her "friend." And you sure didn't start wearing a suit and tie.

"Well, do come in," said Krok, nervously fingering his guitar.

"Would you like something to drink?" stammered Smash.
"Iced tea maybe?"

Behind her rose-tinted monogrammed "U" glasses, Umm's eyes smiled. The way her hair frizzed out, it looked as though grabbing this lady for a one-night cave encounter would only produce a handful of hairspray.

Umm observed the handsome harp man's three hairy friends. It was not a pretty sight. "Sure," she smiled and hoped they could play.

"Umm came to hear us play," said Stone.

"I can dig that," said Smash, "but what's with the suit and tie?"

"Listen, man," said Stone, "it takes more than grime and sweat to make good music. Let's add a little class to the act. Besides, Umm here has got us a gig."

"A gig?" said Krok. "Where?"

Not exactly a gig – an audition," said Umm.
"What's an addition?" asked Smash.
"It's a gig…" offered Stone.
"But you don't get paid," added Gref.
"If they like you, they ask you to come back," said Krok.
"Then they pay you," chimed Stone.

Smash frowned and rubbed his stubby chin. His drumsticks looked like twigs in his huge hands.

"Where is this audition?" asked Krok.

"At 'The Club,'" said Umm. "I know the guy who runs the place."

"Let's practice," Stone said. He loosened his necktie. "I gotta new harp style I want to try. If we're gonna audition, we want to be ready. And look…" he turned to Krok, "this time let's tune up before we play."

"Tune up again?" asked Krok with a shudder. He usually tuned the deer sinew guitar strings about every six months. "What the devil for?"

"So it sounds like we're playing in the same key!" shouted Stone. So an **E** note on your guitar and Gref's bass is the same as an **E** note on my harmonica. So the music doesn't sound like a bunch of Neanderthals banging on pots and pans!"

Krok looked carefully at Stone standing there with his hands on his hips; his suit, loosened tie and "friend" giving him a new air of authority.

Tune up? It had never made any difference before. It was obvious Stone was just trying to impress this frizz-haired Umm. As leader, songwriter and guitarist for the Cave Boys, Krok considered telling Stone to start walking.

But he stopped himself. Good harp players were hard to find. Besides, if he got rid of Stone, he might lose his audition.

"Okay," he finally said to Stone, "give me a note."

Tuning Guitars
to Harmonicas

On those rare occasions when they did tune, the band always matched notes with Stone's harmonica. It was the only instrument around that didn't change pitch. Bass and guitar strings (especially guitar) got out of tune just sitting around. Hot weather made the strings stretch and get lower. Cold weather made them tighten and get higher.

Even Stone's harps got out of tune, though they were certainly more reliable than the string instruments. (See page 209 for harp tuning)

Now, being in tune meant that a certain note on one instrument was the same note on another instrument. The procedure was for Stone to play a note on his harp and for Gref and Krok to tune their instruments to that note.

The guitar strings were set up like this. The first string was tuned to an **E** note. The second one to a **B**, the third to a **G**, the fourth to a **D**, the fifth to an **A**, and the sixth string to an **E**.

Here's how the guitar looked:

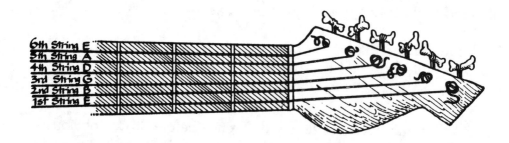

And the bass, a four-stringed instrument, was set up like Krok's guitar. The only difference was that the strings were much thicker and were set down an octave from the guitar.

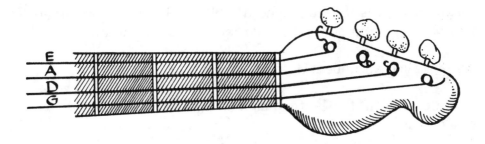

So, on both bass and guitar, the lowest string needed to be tuned to an **E** note. Stone pulled out his **C** harp. The layout of notes looked like this:

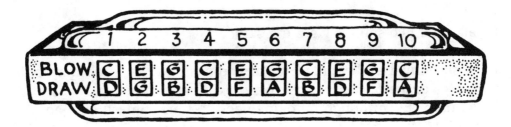

"Gimme an **E**, a low **E**," said Gref.

Stone played a 2 blow on his **C** harp. Bass and guitar strings varoomed as the **E** strings were tightened to play the same note as an **E** on Stone's harmonica.

"Okay, gimme an **A**," said Krok, once his **E** string was in tune.

Stone played a 6 draw, careful not to bend it so Krok and Gref would not be tuning to a flattened note.

Again, bass and guitar strings twanged.

Smash sighed impatiently. Tuning was necessary, he guessed. But it took so long! Why couldn't the band just play and pretend they were in tune?

"How 'bout a **D**?" asked Gref once the **E** and **A** strings on the guitar and bass were the same pitch as the **E** and **A** notes on the harp.

Again careful not to bend the note or cup the harp in his hands, Stone now played a 4 draw on his **C** harp. This was his **D** note.

For the **G** strings, Stone played a 3 blow. Gref was now tuned. His bass had only four strings. But Krok needed a **B** note.

Stone played an unbent 3 draw.

"Varooom!" went the **B** string as it sought out the pitch that would match Stone's **B**.

And for the final note, another **E**, Stone played a higher **E** on his harp: the 5 blow.

Krok carefully tightened the tuning peg, and his high **E** string slid up toward the same pitch as the harp's **E** note.

Finally, the two sounds were the same.

Krok strummed a **C** chord. Gref played a riff on the 1-3-5 harmonizing notes of the **C** scale. Stone played a **C** note, the 4 blow on his **C** harp. Even though he didn't need to tune, Smash banged his drums.

"Guess we're there," said Krok.

"Your **B** string is a little flat," said Umm.

"My what?" Krok could not believe he was hearing this.

"Your **B** string," said Umm, smiling sweetly from her cloud of smoke. "Go ahead, strum your **C** chord again. You'll hear it."

Krok strummed each string on his **C** chord. Sure enough, the **B** did sound slightly out of whack. He tightened the tuning peg.

"Mmmmmmmmmmm," he said to Umm. "Not only pretty but pretty darn smart, if you ask me."

"Why don't you guys play something?" she quietly asked.

"Yeah..." said Smash. He brought his sticks down on his snare drums with a tremendous bang.

Stone Jams Straight Harp

"Okay," said Krok, "let's try that slow love song, 'Cave Angel.' It'll go over good at The Club. Key of **C**. Slow tempo. Guess you'll count four steps from the **C** and play an **F** harmonica," he said to Stone, who was bristling that Krok, a lowly guitarist, was telling him, Stone, the harp man, how to play in front of his new lady, no less.

Stone smiled quietly. "No, I'm gonna do something different on this song. I'm gonna play my **C** harp in the key of **C**. You know... Straight Harp. It sounds more...more..."

"Romantic..." said Umm.

"Yeah, romantic."

Krok squinted at his harp player. Romantic? What had this woman done to him?

"Okay. Here goes," he finally said. "One, two, three, four."

Krok strummed the I chord of "Cave Angel." This was, of course, a **C** chord. Gref added supporting notes on his bass, and Smash played a soft steady rhythm.

Then Krok played an **A** minor chord, the relative minor of the **C** chord. From here the music went into an **F** chord, the IV chord of the progression, then it moved to a **G**, the V chord, and returned to the **C**, the I Chord of Resolution.

Using the relative minor chord, the chord 6 steps up from the I chord, gave the music a more melodic feeling than did the simple I-IV-V progression. Now, the progression went I-VI-IV-V. Although this occurred thousands of years ago, Krok's music sounded remarkably like one of those slow-dance pop ballads that were so popular in the late 1950s and early 60s.

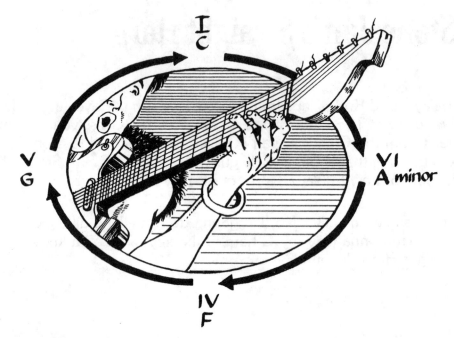

Krok began to sing:

     C   Am   F   G
     "Cave angel, what can I do?
     C   Am   F   G
     To earn your love so true?
     C   Am   F G   C
     Cave angel, will you be mine?"

Umm leaned forward. These guys might look rowdy, but they weren't half bad. The blood began to flow more quickly through her heart.

Meanwhile, Stone was preparing to enter the music. He held his **C** harp to his puckered lips.

He hadn't played Straight Harp with the band before. Normally, he used this harp style for playing melodies around a campfire. He couldn't get down and boogie playing Straight Harp. He couldn't get that bluesy, tension-creating feeling.

Still, on this slow moving, pretty love song, bluesy Cross Harp would be out of place. So Straight Harp it was.

144

Straight Harp Revisited

This is the way Straight Harp works (from a Cave Boy's point of view). Take your **C** harmonica and blow on holes 1234. This is your Straight Harp Blow Chord.

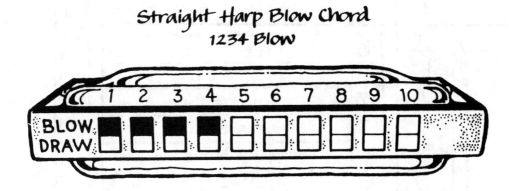

You can also play the Straight Harp Blow Chord by playing holes 4567 blow or 789 and 10 blow. ALL your blow notes are harmonizing notes.

The Notes of Resolution are 1 blow, 4 blow, 7 blow and 10 blow.

The basic approach, then, to playing improvisational Straight Harp is to accent the blow notes, use the draw notes as Stepping Stones (almost the exact opposite of Cross Harp) and to resolve on 1 blow, 4 blow, 7 blow or 10 blow.

Map of Straight Harp

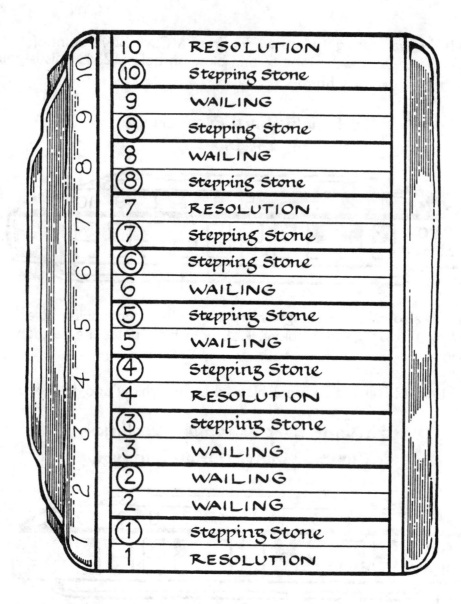

10	RESOLUTION
(10)	Stepping Stone
9	WAILING
(9)	Stepping Stone
8	WAILING
(8)	Stepping Stone
7	RESOLUTION
(7)	Stepping Stone
(6)	Stepping Stone
6	WAILING
(5)	Stepping Stone
5	WAILING
(4)	Stepping Stone
4	RESOLUTION
(3)	Stepping Stone
3	WAILING
(2)	WAILING
2	WAILING
(1)	Stepping Stone
1	RESOLUTION

THE STRAIGHT HARP I CHORD OF RESOLUTION is expressed with single notes 1 blow, 4 blow, 7 blow and 10 blow.

THE IV STEPPING STONE CHORD is expressed with single notes 5 draw, 9 draw and 2 draw bent down.

THE DOMINANT WAILER V CHORD is expressed with single notes 2 draw, 3 blow, 6 blow and 9 blow.

146

As you play Straight Harp, you'll discover that the draw notes – although they're called Stepping Stone Notes – *almost* harmonize. Stepping Stone Notes like 1 draw, 4 draw and 6 draw can be drawn out, accented, as long as a Note of Resolution follows them, or as long as the song isn't on the I chord of the I-IV-V progression.

So, if you're getting clear, single notes, it's pretty hard to make a mistake playing Straight Harp.

Here's a simple Straight Harp Riff that will always harmonize if you are in tune with the guitarist and are playing the right key of harmonica.

Meadow Lark Melody Run
5 ④ 4

You can also play the Meadow Lark Melody Run on the high and low end of your harmonica.

High Meadow Lark Melody Run
8 ⑧ 7

Low Meadow Lark Melody Run
2 ① 1

You can play an Up and Down Meadow Lark Melody Run by returning to the Straight Harp Wailing Note 5 blow immediately after playing the 4 blow.

Up and Down
Meadow Lark Melody Run
5 ④ 4 5   5 ④ 4

High Up and Down
Meadow Lark Melody Run
8 ⑧ 7 8   8 ⑧ 7

147

As mentioned earlier, Straight Harp does not create a bluesy wailing tension in the manner of Cross Harp. And, beneath 7 blow, the blow notes can't be bent.

However, on hole 7 and above, the blow notes *can* be bent. By pushing the airstream forward and down, you can make your 7 blow, 8 blow, 9 blow and 10 blow swoop down. And, by releasing the air you've directed down into your harmonica, you can bring these Straight Harp Harmonizing Notes back to the top of their bending potentials.

For instance, you can create tension on the High Meadow Lark Melody Run by bending the 8 blow Wailing Note.

And, you can resolve the tension with the Straight Harp Descender, a pattern that takes you from Straight Harp Wailing Note 8 blow down to Straight Harp Note of Resolution 4 blow.

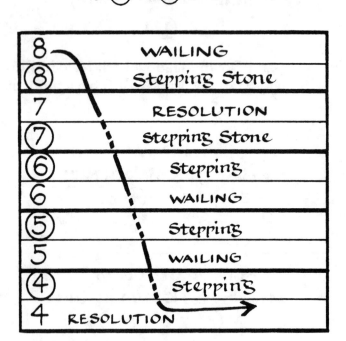

148

From the 4 blow, you can wind your way to the Wailing Note 8 blow.

Straight Harp Ascender
4 ④ 5 6 7 ⑧ 8

8	WAILING
⑧	Stepping
7	RESOLUTION
⑦	Stepping Stone
⑥	Stepping
6	WAILING
⑤	Stepping
5	WAILING
④	Stepping Stone
4	RESOLUTION

These patterns should give you a few ideas for Straight Harp improvisational accompaniment. You can use them as "fillers" – musical phrases that keep a song interesting, or you can use them to create solos. Built on a framework of Straight Harp Harmonizing Notes, the mood and timing of these riffs can be modified to fit the song you're accompanying.

In addition, you can figure out almost all melodies that use a major scale and play them in the Straight Harp Style. The only major scale on your diatonic harp starts on 4 blow and goes:

4 ④ 5 ⑤ 6 ⑥ ⑦ 7
do re mi fa so la ti do

So if your band were going to release a new version of "Old Mac-Donald Had A Farm," you, the harp player, could toot around on this major scale until you discovered the melody.

7   7   7   6   ⑥ ⑥ 6
Old MacDonald had a farm
8   8   ⑧   ⑧   7
Eeeeeyyyy eeeeeyyyy ohhhh

But say the record producer didn't like the way the harp sounded. "C'mon," he says, "You're making this MacDonald guy sound like a pansy. How 'bout some lower, more throaty notes?"

Then you might go searching for the melody on your lower notes – and to your dismay, you'd discover there isn't a complete scale from 1 blow to 4 blow.

You'd find that the *fa* was missing as well as the *la*. You would NOT be able to play the note for the word "had" in those poignant lines, "Old MacDonald had a farm."

4   4   3   ?   3
Old MacDonald had a farm

Panic sets in! Here you are on the verge of a big recording contract – and you can't find the note for "had."

What you need is a major scale from 1 blow to 4 blow. Okay. Here's what you do. There are notes missing between 2 blow and 2 draw and between 3 blow and 3 draw.

The only way to play a major scale is to bend to 2 draw down before playing the unbent 2 draw, and to bend the 3 draw down before playing the unbent 3 draw.

1   ①   2   ②** ②   ③** ③   4
do re mi fa so la ti do

150

The note you'd need for playing the "had" in "Old MacDonald" would be the 3 draw bent down.

$$4 \quad 4 \quad 3 \quad ③^{**} \quad 3$$
Old MacDonald had a farm
$$5 \quad 5 \quad ④ \quad ④ \quad 4$$
Eeeeeyyyy eeeeeyyyy ohhh

"Perfect!" cries the producer. "You're going to go a long ways with this little tune!"

So, to enhance your ability in playing Straight Harp melodies, practice this major scale starting from 1 blow.

$$1 \quad ① \quad 2 \quad ②^{**} \quad ② \quad ③^{**} \quad ③ \quad 4$$
do re mi fa so la ti do

And also learn to play the major scale going from 4 blow to 1 blow.

$$4 \quad ③ \quad ③^{**} \quad ② \quad ②^{**} \quad 2 \quad ① \quad 1$$
do ti la so fa mi re do

This may be the most difficult technique in the entire book. Still, when "Old MacDonald" strikes it big and your group has started a whole new musical genre, "Punk Nursery Rhymes," don't forget where you learned it.

~~~

But let's get back to Stone, standing there in the musty cave, sweating like Niagara in his suit and loosened tie, **C** harp to his lips as the Cave Boys enter another cycle of this old *be bop* chord progression.

Stone tongues his 4 blow. He slides the harp to 5 blow and plays the Meadow Lark Melody Run: 5 blow, 4 draw, 4 blow. He wails on the 8 blow, slips up to the 9 blow and wails there. Back to the 8 blow, bending the note and releasing it. Then the 8 Blow Descender – 8 blow, 8 draw, 7 blow, 6 draw, 6 blow, 5 blow, 4 blow – hitting that

Straight Harp Note of Resolution at exactly the moment the chord progression has gone full cycle and resolves on the I chord.

It sounds so good, Krok almost drops his guitar. His monkey suited harpist has created a spell with his sensitive Straight Harp. Krok closes his eyes and begins to sing.

"I'd take a bath, I'd comb my hair." A soft 8 blow reverberates off the cave walls. "To show you how much I care." The 8 blow curves down and seems to fall through space as Stone plays the 8 Draw Descender. "Cave angel, will you be mine?" The harmonica echoes the voice with the Meadow Lark Melody run. *Wa wa wa!* the 4 blow actually cries.

"Cave angel...." *Wa wa wa*
"Cave angel...." *Wa wa wa*
"Cave angel...." *Wa wa wa*
"Cave angel...." Only this time the voice doesn't belong to Krok. No, Krok's voice is halfway between a belch and a grunt. This voice is rich, expressive. It belongs to Umm. She's standing up, hands clenched to her bosom, eyes closed, mouth open.

"Cave angel, will you be mine?"

The entire cave seems to be swinging back and forth to this sad, gut wrenching melody. Umm's voice is like a musical instrument. The harp punctuates the music, underscores the emotion. Smash keeps a steady beat. Gref's bass is supportive, sensitive.

Finally, the song ends. The musicians are exhausted, but amazed. This girl can sing! Smash is the first to speak.

"Wow! A chick singer!"

Umm glares, "A woman vocalist."

"Well, guys?" Stone asks, "Can she join our band?"

"We couldn't call ourselves the Cave Boys," says Gref.

"Yeah," says Smash, "It would seem funny."

152

Umm looks at the four musicians. These guys weren't bad. And they were nice enough. Dumb, true. But at least they got into the music. Should she? Well, why not?

"I've got an idea," she says, "How 'bout Umm and the Cave Boys?"

"Sounds good to me," grins Stone.

"I like it," says Gref. "What do you think, Krok?"

All eyes turn to guitarist, songwriter and lead singer of the band. "Well, what do you think?"

No answer. But in Krok's mind, the possibilities are spinning like peaches and cherries on a slot machine. First, they get the job at The Club. Then they move on, playing Dinosaur Breath a couple of nights a week (it's a nice little dive near the tar pits), and then maybe to the big time. Money, booze, women…and maybe, just maybe, Umm, too.

He eyes the frizzy-haired phenomenon standing across the cave. Firelight flickers in her hair, sparkles in her "U" monogrammed glasses, throws shadows on her high, delicate cheekbones.

"Well, tell me this," he says, "How are you at singing rock and blues?"

With that Umm opens her mouth and shouts-sings-laughs-cries, "Baby, why you treat me like you do? Whyyyy? Whyyyy? Whyyyy?"

"Oh yeah!" grunts the voice in Krok's head. "Oh yeah!"

He can see it now. Las Vegas. New York. Los Angeles. World tours. Cosmic tours. Records. Royalties. Revenge on all the people who said he'd never make it. And all because of Umm, this sweet little chick singer, Umm.

"Well," he finally says, "Your voice needs work, but I'll spend some extra time working with you."

"Whooopppppppeeeeeee!" shouts Smash.

And that is how Stone's Straight Harp added diversity and class to a ragged old band that never would have made it out of the cave.

"Incidentally," said Umm, "I think your **B** string is still a little flat."

Notes

* Two instruments that aren't tuned to each other sound lousy when played at the same time.

* Being IN TUNE means that an **E** note on the guitar is the same as an **E** note on a harp. Ditto for **A, D, G, B** or any other note.

* The guitar tunes to the harmonica. The harp player gives the guitarist a note and tells him or her what note it is. On an **E** harp, 1 blow is an **E**. On a **D** harp, 1 blow is a **D**. On a **G** harp, 1 blow is a **G**.

* On your **C** harmonica, 2 blow and 5 blow are **E** notes. Use the major scale chart on page 141 to figure out where other important guitar tuning notes are located.

* To play the Straight Harp style of harmonica, play a **C** harp in the key of **C**, a **G** harp in the key of **G**, a **D** harp in the key of **D**. Accent the blow notes. Use draw notes as Stepping Stones.

* Playing Straight Harp, the Notes of Resolution are 1 blow, 4 blow, 7 blow and 10 blow.

NINE

Campfire Melodies Played Cross Harp

*Umm, Stone, Krok, Gref and Smash vacation in the mountains.
Stone goes nuts turning some old songs into tasty blues melodies.
The band loves it, and so will you.*

A Circle of Friends

The vacationing band sat around the campfire. The descent of the sun had turned the horizon from blue to purple, and the first stars of the evening were taking a bow in a theatre of clear skies.

Krok threw a log on the fire and a shower of sparks made everyone move. Umm told a joke about smoke keeping away the mosquitos. The laughter and talk drifted into a contented silence. Only the fire seemed lively, snapping and crackling, drawing all eyes into a kaleidoscope of blue and orange warmth.

As the sky darkened, Stone and his friends leaned closer to the glowing logs. The harp man took his harmonica from his pocket and started to softly play.

"Wa wa wa waaaaaa!"

His simple Cross Harp riffs kept beat to the crackling of flame and wood. A jug of wine made its way around the fire, passed hand to hand, hand to mouth.

Krok placed some dry wood on the fire and Stone's harmonica energy rose with the flame. So did the energy of his circle of friends. Smash grunted after a particularly soulful phrase out of Stone's boo boo reed harmonica, and Gref couldn't stop himself from dancing.

The party had started. The fire danced to the singing harmonica, crackling and popping its feisty percussion, castanets on fingers of flame. The wine made its sloshing way around the fire once more. Stone brought his music to a close.

"Don't stop" said a shadowy face across the fire. It was Umm. "Play some more," she urged. "Play something we can all sing."

"Yeah!" said Smash, carried away by the beauty of the moment. "Play uh, 'Red River Valley.' You know, that old cowboy song. Everybody knows it."'

"Play 'Frankie and Johnnie,'" said Gref.

"Play 'Shortnin' Bread,'" giggled Umm.

Stone looked at his friends through his hands. Did they really want him to play such hokey old Straight Harp songs? He'd graduated from that long ago! Then he had an idea! He'd play the tunes blues style, 2nd position. The hard part would be bending the 2 draw and 3 draw to hit the notes at 2 draw** and 3 draw**. But what the heck, it would be good practice! He'd really start to understand melody!

Plus, he'd be able to improvise by sticking riffs between the pauses of the songs. Man, this would blow their minds!

Shyly at first, Stone started to play. Once they got the hang of Stone's bluesy approach, Gref and Smash started to sing along, matched by Umm's wailing cave girl howls. Even Krok, who was often embarrassed by innocence and fun began singing along in his rough hewn voice. Then he grabbed his backpacking guitar and began strumming the chords.

"Hey!" he shouted, "these old songs sound good when you play 'em blues style!"

Cross Harp Camp Fire Music

Stoney started with this old favorite played in 2nd position. Reason? It turned this old cowboy song into a cowboy blues song. He played it through the first time as written. The second time, he decided to improvise on the melody. The basic idea is that instead of playing the melody in the underlined spots, you play a blues riff that ends on the same note that the melody ends on.

RED RIVER VALLEY BLUES 2nd position

G
①　②　③　•　•　•　③**　③　③**　②
From this val ley they say you are go ing

①　②　③　②　③　④　4　③　③**　D7
We will miss your bright eyes and sweet smile

G　　　　　　　　　　　　　　C
④　4　③　•　③**　②　③**　③　④　4
For they say you are tak ing the sun shine

D7　　　　　　　　　　　　　　　G　C　G
①　•　•　②*　②　③**　③　③**　②
Which has brightened our path for a while

Improvisation Ideas

6　⑤　5　④　③　③**②　•
you oo oo oo are go ing

5　④　5　④　or ③** or ⑥
and sweet smile

⑥　•　6　⑤　④　•　•　③　4　•
For they say you are tak ing the sun shine

④　5　③　•　③**②
ened our path for a while

While Krok strummed guitar in a basic blues progression (chords included), Stone first caressed a bluesy version of "Red River" followed by "Sunshine." The second time through on both songs, he improvised by jumping to the high end and integrating blues riffs with pieces of the established melodies.

160

YOU ARE MY SUNSHINE BLUES 2nd position

No Chord   G7   G7

(1)   (2)   (3)**   (3)   •   (3)   (3)**   (3)   (2)   •

You   are   my   sun shine. My   on   ly   sun shine

         C7   G7

(2)   (3)**   (3)   4   5   5   (4)   4   (3)

You make me   hap py   when   skies are   grey

         C7   G7   C7

(2)   (3)**   (3)   4   5   5   (4)   4   (3)   (2)

You'll   ne   ver know dear how much I   love   you

G7   D7   G7

(2)   (3)**   (3)   4   (3)**   •   (3)   (2)

Please don't take my   sun shine   a   way

YOU ARE MY SUNSHINE BLUES 2nd position (high end)

(4)   6   (6)   (7)   •   (7)   (6)   (7)   6   •

You   are   my   sun shine. My   on   ly   sun shine

6   (6)   (7)   7   8   •   (8)   7   (7)

You make me   hap py   when   skies are   grey

6   (6)   (7)   7   8   8   (8)   7   (7)   6

You'll   ne   ver know dear how much I   love   you

6   (6)   (7)   7   (6)   •   (7)   6

Please don't take my   sun shine   a   way

Improvisations for the high end

9   (9)   8   (8)   (7)   (6)   6

my   on------------------ly   sun shine

(2)   (3)** (3)   4   5   5   (4)   4   (3)

You make me   hap   py   when skies are   grey

(6)   (7)   (6)

(insert this quick riff between "love" and "you".)

161

JOSHUA FOUGHT THE BATTLE 3rd position–C harp in D minor

(4) • 5 • (5) • 6 (6) (5) (6)
Jos hua fought the bat tle of Jer i cho,

6 5 6 (6) (5) (6)
Jer i cho, Jer i cho

(4) • 5 • (5) • 6 (6) (5) (6)
Jos hua fought the bat tle of Jer i cho,

(4) 5 (6) 6 (5) 5 (4)
And the walls came tum bling down

JOSHUA FOUGHT THE BATTLE 4th position–C harp in A minor

(3)** • (3) • 4 • (4) 5 4 5
Jos hua fought the bat tle of Jer i cho,

(4) (3) (4) 5 4 5
Jer i cho, Jer i cho

(3)** • (3) • 4 • (4) 5 4 5
Jos hua fought the bat tle of Jer i cho,

4 (4) 5 (4) 4 (3) (3)**
And the walls came tum bling down

JOSHUA FOUGHT THE BATTLE 5th position–C harp in E minor

2 • (2)** • (2) • (3)** (3) (2) (3)
Jos hua fought the bat tle of Jer i cho,

(3)** (2)** (3)** (3) (2) (3)
Jer i cho, Jer i cho

2 • (2)** • (2) • (3)** (3) (2) (3)
Jos hua fought the bat tle of Jer i cho,

(2) (3)** (3) (3)** (2) (2)** 2
And the walls came tum bling down

Now Stone did something that blew his own mind, not to mention his incredulous band mates. Somehow, he wandered into position-playing (see page 199) and played "Jericho" in three different minor keys. He had no idea what he was doing, but man, did it sound good.

SHORTNIN' BREAD 2nd position

Fast G7 Strum

② • 5 • ④ • 5 ② 5 ④ 5
Mam my's lit- tle ba- by loves short nin', short nin'

② • 5 • ④ • 5 ③ ③** ②
Mam my's lit- tle ba- by loves short nin' bread   (repeat)

6 • 5 ④ 5 6 • 5 ④
Put on the skil let, put on the lid

6 • 5 • ④ • 5 • ③ ③** ②
Mam my gon na bake a lit- tle short-nin' bread

6 5 ④ 5 6 5 ④
That ain't all she's gon na do

6 • 5 • ④ • 6 • ③ ③** ②
Mam my gon na make a lit tle cof fee too

AMAZING GRACE 12th position—C harp in key of F

F   B   F
4 ⑤ ⑥ ⑥ 6 ⑤ ④ 4
A maz ing grace, how sweet the sound

F   B   C
④ ⑤ ⑥ ⑥ 6 7
That saved a wretch like me

F   B   F
⑥ 7 ⑥ ⑤ ⑥ 6 ⑤ ④ 4
I once was lost, but now am found

F   B   F
4 ④ ⑤ ⑥ ⑥ 6 ⑤
Was blind, but now I see

Arranged by John McLaughlin, Seattle, WA

Stone could do no wrong. Everything he played was golden, including this amazingly easy and expressive version of "Amazing Grace," played 12th position, C harp in the key F. "That's the best version yet," sighed Umm as she came closer. Stone hoped that somehow he'd remember what he had just played.

BILL BAILEY 2nd position

G7
③ • ③** ③ ③** ③ ④
Won't you come home Bill Bai -ley?

③ • ③** ③
Won't you come home?

D7
④ • ③ ④ 5 ③**
She cried the whole night long.

D7
4 • ③* 4 ③ 4 ④ 4 • ③ 4
I'll do the dish es ba by, I'll pay the rent,

G7
④ 5 ④ 5 • ③
I know I done you wrong.

G7
③ • • ③** ③ ③** ③ ④ ③ • ③** ③
Remember that rai ny even-ing, I drove you out

C7
6 • • • • ⑥ 6 5
with noth ing but a fine tooth comb

C7   G7   E7
6 • • 5 6 5 ④ • 5 ③
I know I'm to blame. Well, ain't that a shame.

A7   D7   G   G7
③ • ③** ③ ③** ④ ③ ②
Bill Bai ley won't you please come home?

This was Stone's chance to really exercise the 3 draw tongue bends and unbends. Nose closed, nose open, closed, open. Instead of huffing and puffing, he compressed his airstream to get more power from less effort, using the drawn "ta" to give each bend a sharp attack and yet play under extreme control. When he arrived at the treacherous 3 draw** for the word "long," he went right to the bend, played it spot on, and got off before it could waver.

164

FRANKIE AND JOHNNIE BLUES 2nd position

G7   C7   G7

② ③** ③ 5 ④ 5 ② •

Frank ie and John nie were lov ers

G7   C7   G7

② ③** ③ 5 ④ 5 ②

Oh Lord -y how they could love

C7

6 • ④ 5 ④ 6 • • ④ 6

They swore to   be   true to each oth er

                          G7

6 • • ④ 5 ④

True as the stars a -bove

                D7

③ ④ 5 ④

He was her man,

C7   G7 D7

④ • • 4 3 ③* ②

But he was do ing her wrong.

Improvisational ideas

⑤ •

lov ers

⑤

love

5 6 ⑥ 6 ⑥ 6 5 ④ 5

They swore to be true to each oth er

② • • ③ ④ 5 ④

True as the   stars a- bove

⑤

man

6 ⑤ 5 ④ 3 • ②

But he was do ing her wrong

A blues murder ballad! Smash even knew the words. In his surprisingly squeaky voice, he sang the lines and Stone's harp repeated them.

"Frankie and Johnny went walking
John in his brand new suit
'My, oh my,' said Frankie girl
Don't my Johnny Boy look cute!"
He was her man...(chorus)

"Frankie looked over the transom
much to her surprise
There was her Johnny boy
Loving up Alice Bly" He was...

"Frankie drew back her kimono
pulled out her little .44
Rat ta tat! three times she shot
Right through that hardwood
floor!" He was...

"The judge said to the jury, It's plain as plain can be
That woman shot poor Johnny. It's murder in the second degree
He was her man, but he was doing her wrong."

WHEN THE SAINTS GO MARCHING IN 1st position

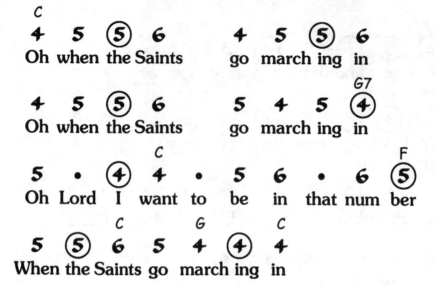

C
4　5　⑤　6　　　　4　5　⑤　6
Oh when the Saints　　go march ing in

4　5　⑤　6　　　　5　4　5　④
Oh when the Saints　　go march ing in　　[G7]

C
5　•　④　4　•　5　6　•　6　⑤
Oh Lord　I　want　to　be　in　that num ber　[F]

C　　　　　G　　　　C
5　⑤　6　5　4　④　4
When the Saints go march ing in

WHEN THE SAINTS GO MARCHING IN 2nd position

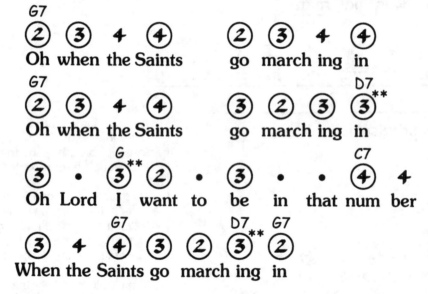

G7
②　③　4　④　　　　②　③　4　④
Oh when the Saints　　go march ing in

G7
②　③　4　④　　　　③　②　③　③**
Oh when the Saints　　go march ing in　　[D7]

G
③　•　③**　②　•　③　•　•　④　4
Oh Lord　I　want　to　be　in　that num ber　[C7]

G7　　　　　D7　G7
③　4　④　③　②　③**　②
When the Saints go march ing in

For his evening's finale, Stone started off with a simple Straight Harp version of "Saints." After the verse, he went right into a long wailing 4 draw **tata tata tata** that he renewed three times, creating unbearable tension, and then slid down to the 1234 draw chord where he drove the rhythm to a train-like frenzy, and finally played the 2 draw lead to the same song, now Cross Harp. He filled the pauses with riffs of lightning, reveling in the joy of changing keys to make a song unforgettable. Only problem was, no one but Stone heard it. The rest of the band had fallen asleep hours earlier.

166

Transposing 1st Position Songs to 2nd Position

Most harmonica notation for traditional and pop songs is in 1st position. The reason is that 1st position is easier. However, most players find it far less soulful. This chart will help you transpose trite 1st position songs into 2nd position blues and country masterpieces.*

If a song starts on 4 blow in 1st position, in 2nd position it will begin on 2 draw or 3 blow. If it moves from the 4 blow to a 5 blow in the Straight Harp version, then the Cross Harp version will move from a 3 blow to 3 draw unbent.

If a 1st position song uses this note	Use one of these notes to play it in 2nd position
② 3 6 9	① ④ ⑧
1 4 7	② 3 6 9
2 5 8	③ ⑦ ⑨
③* ⑦*	②** ⑤
③ ⑦	②* 9*
① ④ ⑧	③** ⑥
②** ⑤	1 4 7 10
③** ⑥	2 5 8
C Harp Key of C	C Harp Key of G

*To play Cross Harp melodies in the Nashville style of Charlie McCoy, one would use a country-tuned harmonica. This special tuning has the 5 draw filed to play a half step up.

TEN

Third Position Slant Harp A Big Time Harp Style

Slant Harp is the style of harmonica many harpists use to accompany songs in Minor Keys. Most appropriate for blues and rock, Slant Harp uses 4 draw as a Note of Resolution.

In Chapter X, Stone makes a television appearance, discovers the secrets of Slant Harp, and finally understands the purpose of musical artistry.

Stone Looks for a New Harp Style

"There has to be a way. There has to be..." Stone was walking down the mountainside, muttering to himself. His feet slipped on the trailside rocks, and once he even ran into a tree, but the harp-playing Cave Boy barely noticed his own clumsiness. He was bummed.

This had never happened to Stone before. He had ALWAYS been able to provide great accompaniment to any song Umm and the Cave Boys played.

But Krok's new tune, a reggae-flavored ditty called "Volcano Mouth," was giving him trouble. The song was in the key of **A** minor, and for some reason, neither Cross nor Straight Harp sounded very good.

Making matters worse, today was the day of the television appearance. The Cave Boys were scheduled to play on the Dinah Sledgehammer Show, and Krok wanted to introduce "Volcano Mouth" to the fans.

"Listen," he had said to Stone. "If you can't figure out what to play, then don't. No harmonica sounds better than lousy harmonica." Krok had put his arm protectively around Umm's shoulder. "Besides, you wouldn't want to do anything to harm Umm's career, would you?"

"Oh, c'mon," Umm had said, wriggling away from Krok. "It doesn't sound *that bad*."

Doesn't sound that bad, Stone had repeated to himself. *Doesn't sound that bad*. The purpose of his playing was to sound great. No one had ever said *doesn't sound that bad* about his harp-playing before.

"Hey!" he had sputtered, "I'll figure out something. Ol' Harp Boy Stone can play anything." His nervous laugh had been cut off by Krok's abrupt remark. "Why not just bang a tambourine? We've got harmonica on too many songs already."

Now, walking down the mountain trail to the theatre where the show was to be held, Stone brooded over his problem. Playing songs in minor keys had never troubled him before. A minor chord was only a slight variation of a major chord.

Instead of playing the 1st, 3rd and 5th notes of a major scale to form a major chord, what Krok did was strum the 1st, flatted 3rd and 5th notes. This resulted in a minor chord.

To accompany, Stone would ask what key the song was in. If Krok answered "**A** minor," Stone would count four steps up the scale from **A** (including the **A**).

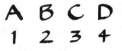

He'd play Cross Harp on a **D** harmonica. The one rule he had to follow to play Cross Harp in a minor key: he had to play the 3 draw slightly bent. The unbent 3 draw clashed.

Another approach was to play Straight Harp. If the song were in the key of **A** minor, he would count up 3 steps to figure out that **A** minor was the relative minor of the **C** chord. He would then play Straight Harp on a **C** harmonica.

If the song were in **D** minor, he'd count up 3 steps and play an **F** harmonica in the Straight Harp style.

D E F
1 2 3

But on "Volcano Mouth" neither Straight nor Cross Harp were worth beans. They didn't follow the tune. It sounded as though he were trying to wedge riffs into spots where they didn't belong. What was he going to do?

Now, with the rock facade of the theatre clearly in sight, Stone's mind started working with desperate energy. What he needed was a new harp style. All the styles he had learned so far were based on the locations of the Notes of Resolution.

For instance, playing Cross Harp, the Notes of Resolution were 2 draw, 3 blow, 6 blow, 9 blow, and, of course, the Cross Harp Draw Chord, holes 1234 drawn at the same time. Blowing Straight Harp, the Notes of Resolution were 1 blow, 4 blow, 7 blow, 10 blow and holes 1234 blown at the same time. Hmmm, he thought, Maybe... just maybe...

Stone placed his **G** harp to his puckered lips and played a 4 draw. Then he played 5 blow, 5 draw, and back to 4 draw. "That's it!" he said aloud. "That's it! USE 4 DRAW AS A NOTE OF RESOLUTION."

His heart beating to the joyous rhythm of making a new discovery, Stone walked around the back of the theatre and sat himself down near some garbage cans. For the next hour, the Cave Boy harmonicist played and learned as much as possible about his new harp style, the style he would call SLANT HARP. Only later, in the 20th century, would it become known as 3rd position (aka double-crossed).

172

The Slant Harp Approach

Slant Harp is a rock and blues style that gives riffs and solos a slightly different feeling than Cross or Straight Harp. It creates a sound that is partly bluesy, partly melodic. It creates a MINOR KEY FEELING.

The Slant Harp Formula is to play a harp in the key that is two steps down the scale from the key the guitarist is playing in. For instance, if the guitarist is playing in the key of **E** minor, count back two steps (including the **E**), and play a **D** harp.

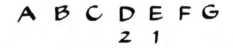

And if the song is in the key of **A** minor, count back two steps from the **A**, and play a **G** harp.

D E F G A B C
2 1

This formula, of course, holds true for any minor key the guitarist chooses to play in.

Once playing the correct key of harmonica, all the Slant Harpist has to do is play riffs and patterns that use 1 draw, 4 draw and 8 draw as Notes of Resolution.

Slant Harp Notes of Resolution
1 Draw, 4 Draw, 8 Draw

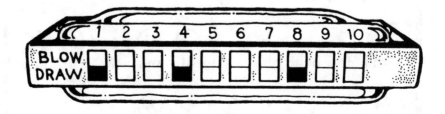

The Slant Harp Wailing Notes are harmonizing notes that will not make a mistake at any point in the minor key variation of the I-IV-V chord progression.

Slant Harp Wailing Notes
5 Draw, 6 Draw, 9 Draw, 10 Draw

Usually, Stepping Stone Notes can be used as rungs on ladders between one harmonizing note and another. But playing Slant Harp, there are three Stepping Stone Notes that will clash with the music no matter how brief a time they are played. These notes to avoid are 2 draw, 3 blow and 3 draw.

The advanced Slant Harpist can bend 2 draw and 3 draw, and turn them into Wailing Notes. However, as mentioned earlier the beginner should stick to holes 4 draw and above. Because Slant Harp is played on the high end of the harp, it's good to start out on the lower-keyed harmonicas such as **G, A, B** or **C**.

SAMPLE SONG: HOUSE OF THE RISING SUN

④　•　5　⑤　⑥　6　④　•
There　is　a　house　in　New　Orleans

⑧　•　•　7　⑥　•
They　call　the　ris　ing　sun

⑧　•　•　•　7　⑥　⑥　6　⑤　④
And　it's　been　the　ruin　of　ma　ny　a　boy

④　•　⑤　6　⑥　4　④
And　Lord　I　know I'm　one

Map of Slant Harp

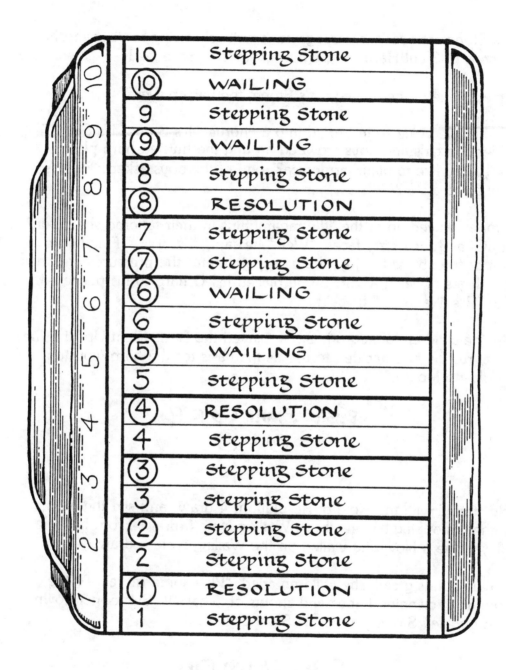

Three draw will clash, unless it's played bent. Then, it's very cool. Playing 3rd Position, 4 blow is a flatted 7th, a powerful Stepping Stone note you should try.

Slant Harp Riffs

As Stone sat near the garbage cans furiously trying to discover the secrets of Slant Harp, a group of children approached.

"Hey!" one of them cried, "it's Stone, the harp player."

The single voice soon turned into a chorus. "It's Stone. It's Stone!" Then the girls and boys crowded aroung the hurried harp player. "What's it like to play harmonica?" one of the boys asked. "What's it like to be a star?"

Stone glanced up at the little ragamuffins in their tattered sheepskin tunics and their dirty faces. "Well," he said, it's, it's..." Finding no words to express the joy, the disappointment, the pressures and the privileges of being a star, Stone placed his **G** harp to his puckered lips. "It's like this..." he said.

As the children looked on, Stone played the Basic Slant Up Riff, the easy run he had decided to use as the basis for the harp work on "Volcano Mouth."

Basic Slant Up Riff
④ ⑤ 6 ⑥

He started with the Note of Resolution, 4 draw, and slid the harp, without stopping his breath, to Wailing Note 5 draw. From here he played the 6 blow and wailed on the Wailing Note 6 draw.

"That sounds great!" the children cried. "Play some more!" To the sounds of clapping hands and shouts of "That's it, Stone, get down and boogie!" Stone played the Slant Down Riff.

Slant Down Riff
⑥ 6 ⑤④

"Yeah!" the kids shouted, "Get it on, Stone!" As Stone continued exploring the possibilities of Slant Harp, a little boy, no longer able to contain himself, started dancing. The other children formed a circle and clapped their hands.

Here are some of the Slant Harp Riffs Stone played. They are presented in diagrams so that, hopefully, you will play them, too.

To start out, Stone played the Ultra Slant Up and Down Riff. This run used the same idea as the Basic Slant, but enhanced the minor key sound even more.

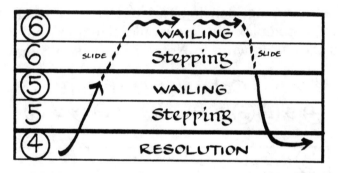

Then Stone moved up an octave and played the Basic Slant Up and Down Riff on holes 8, 9 and 10.

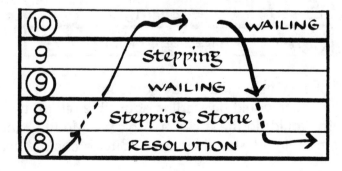

Now he switched to the Ultra Slant Up and Down Riff on holes 8, 9 and 10.

Ultra Slant Up and Down Riff (High Octave)
⑧ 8 ⑨ ⑩ ⑩ ⑨ 8 ⑧

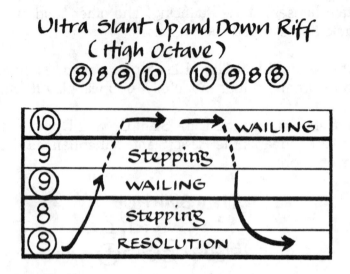

Amidst the handclapping, dancing and laughing, Stone decided to try an even more complex run. He would play a riff that went from Note of Resolution 4 draw up to Note of Resolution 8 draw.

Octave Slant Run
④ 5 ⑤ ⑥ 7 ⑧ ⑧ 7 ⑥ ⑤ 5 ④

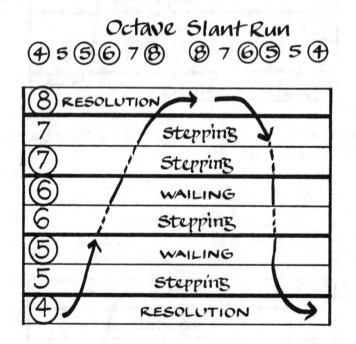

"That's great!" the kids shouted. "Play some more." Stone looked at his watch. The show would be starting soon. He felt pretty confident that Slant Harp would do the trick on "Volcano Mouth," and he knew it was time to get inside the studio. But he couldn't tear himself away from the crowd of girls and boys who now were dancing with their hands in the air, their faces beaming.

"This is it," Stone thought. "This is why I wanted to be a good harmonica player. Not to become a star, not to become famous and make lots of money. No. I learned to play harp so I could bring joy and happiness into the world. So I could help people forget their problems. So I could make them feel good."

Inspired by this realization, Stone played the ultimate Slant Harp riff: the Slant Harp Scale.

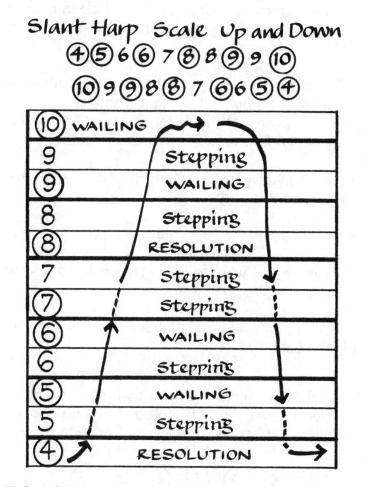

Slant Harp Scale Up and Down
④⑤ 6 ⑥ 7 ⑧ 8 ⑨ 9 ⑩
⑩ 9 ⑨ 8 ⑧ 7 ⑥ 6 ⑤ ④

⑩ WAILING	
9	Stepping
⑨	WAILING
8	Stepping
⑧	RESOLUTION
7	Stepping
⑦	Stepping
⑥	WAILING
6	Stepping
⑤	WAILING
5	Stepping
④	RESOLUTION

"Oh, wow!" the children shouted. "Wowwwwwww!"

Now Stone wanted to really get down and play. Starting from the 4 draw, he played a long bending Note of Resolution, slipped to the 5 draw, the 6 blow, the 6 draw – wailing, warbling, tonguing, bending...

Then, the back door to the theatre suddenly opened, and the gruff face of the theatre manager appeared from the darkness. "Hey! You kids!" he shouted, "you get out of here or I'll call the police! You're making so much noise they can hear you inside." Then he spied Stone sitting beside the garbage cans. "And you, you old bum!" he spat at the greatest harp player who ever lived, "you get out of here, too. Shame on you for making these kids misbehave."

"But that's Stone!" a little girl shouted breathlessly. "That's the harp player for Umm and the Cave Boys."

The theatre manager moved closer. Catching a clearer glimpse of Stone's famous face, the theatre manager turned more colors than a smoggy sunset.

"Excuse me, Mr. Stone," he said, gruff voice now reduced to a whimpering falsetto. "I thought...I thought...oh well...you'd better come in right away. Everyone's looking for you. The show's about to start. Please, c'mon in. Please..."

Stone rose from his place behind the smelly cans. "And what about them?" he asked, pointing at the kids.

"What about them?" the manager asked.

"I want to play for them. I want to know I'm doing some good with all of this superstar hoopla."

"Well..." the theatre manager said. "I guess they can sit in the empty seats in the balcony."

"Whoopee!" the children shouted. And at that moment, Stone played a riff so good it surprised even him. He looked at his boo boo reed beauty in amazement. It was the **3rd Position Low End Scale**.

$$\overset{}{④} \quad 4 \quad \overset{**}{③} \quad ② \quad \overset{**}{②} \quad 2 \quad ①$$

$$① \quad 2 \quad \overset{**}{②} \quad ② \quad \overset{**}{③} \quad 4 \quad ④$$

"What the heck," said the manager, obviously moved, "they can sit at the edge of the stage."

180

The Show

The theatre's back stage was not as nice as the alley. The air was hot and stale, filled with the smells of sweat and makeup, B.O. and cologne.

"Right this way, Mr. Stone," said the theatre manager as he led the harp player past a line of scantily-dressed chorus girls. "Right this way."

Suddenly, Umm rushed up out of the darkness. "Stone!" she cried. She threw her arms around the harp man's neck. "Oh Stone, I was afraid you weren't going to show up. Listen, I don't care how your harp sounds. You're an important member of the Cave Boys. If you don't play, I don't sing."

Stone looked at her in surprise. "I thought nothing was more important to you than your career."

"You're just as important," Umm said. "And don't you forget it."

"You can say that again," added a familiar voice. It was Krok, holding his guitar. Behind him stood Gref and Smash.

"Hey," said Krok, "I'm sorry I got so uptight. This band wasn't any good 'til you joined it. You're playing harp with us – whether you want to or not."

"That's the way I feel too," said Gref.

"Me, too," added Smash.

"Okay," said the manager, "enough of this emotion stuff. What's that have to do with rock and roll? You guys are ON!"

As the manager stepped to the side, the curtains rolled back and Stone suddenly realized that he was standing in front of 5,000 whistling, cheering people. As the cameras moved in, Dinah Sledgehammer was saying, "And now, the group you've been waiting for, Umm and the Cave Boys."

Krok approached the microphone. "We wanna play a new song for you. This is 'Volcano Mouth.'"

The Cave Boy guitarist rose his hand in a wide arc and brought it down on the **A** minor chord. The bass and drums kicked in. The rhythm had a jungle pulse, a primeval beat that made the bones shiver. Wearing a black and gold tiger fur mini dress, Umm danced across the stage. Hair swirling through the air, she grabbed the microphone and started to sing.

"Volcano mouth, volcano mouth
Your mouth is exploding!
　　　　exploding!
　　　　exploding!
Yeahhhhhhhhhhhhhhhh!"

The people in the audience looked at one another. What was this music? What did it mean? Some folks stood up and waved their arms. Others actually moved their hips, thighs, shoulders and hands to the infectious rhythm. Krok nodded at Stone, and the harp man started to put what he had learned about Slant Harp into practice.

He wailed on 4 draw, slipped easily to 8 draw, back to 4 draw. He bent the 4 draw down, brought it back up, slid to 6 draw, blew on 7, sucked on 8, cascaded down to 4 draw in a minor key swirl of sound. His music was perfect for "Volcano Mouth."

Umm, Krok, Gref and Smash looked at Stone with relief and amazement. It was one thing to tell the Cave Boy harp player that he was more important to them than fame and success – quite another to believe it. But now they did believe it. Stone and his harmonica were incredible!

"Oh yeah!" the people in the audience shouted. This was the kind of music they'd always wanted to hear. Umm danced across the stage, whipping the mike cord behind her. Krok dipped to one knee and strummed his chords with robot-like precision. Gref and Smash grinned at one another and Stone wailed like a cave boy possessed.

What a show!

As the audience watched this spectacle of sound and movement, many found themselves thinking that Umm and the Cave Boys were like gods. Gods with the power to turn noise into music, silence into joy, boredom into excitement. And if not gods, then Umm and the Cave Boys were stars, stars as bright and beautiful as any in the heavens.

Few members of the audience realized they were watching the fruits of a long and often tedious labor, that Umm and the Cave Boys were like anyone else, that they fought and got angry with one another, that they were haunted by fears, frustrations, and deep, undefined yearnings for love and acceptance.

Fewer still realized that this vulnerability, this *humanity*, combined with a love for music, a capacity for joy and a need for self-expression, was the source of the magic that now filled the stage and seeped out into their lives. And almost no one was aware that the people themselves also were gods, goddesses, stars, heroes, heroines, what-have-you. No, the music was far too hot and the show too good for this kind of philosophizing.

Stone finished his solo to a standing ovation. Smash's drums rolled and thumped, stampeding the music into the second verse. The lyrics of the second verse were no more profound than those of the first. But who cared? All *anyone* heard was the pounding rhythm, the rich texture of Umm's voice, the razor-sharp slashes of Krok's guitar, the throbbing cry of Stone's harmonica.

Then, as quickly as the magic had begun, it stopped. The song was over. Band members hugged and shook hands. Applause washed over them like tumultuous waves of love.

"Umm and the Cave Boys!" Dinah Sledgehammer was shouting. "Umm and the Cave Boys!"

Krok grasped Stone's hand and looked him in the eye.

"Hey, man," he said, "that was the most incredible harp solo I ever heard you play."

The two musicians stood on the stage, the glow of their mutual success cutting through the rivalries, the arguments, the ego trips that had, for years, kept them from realizing how much they meant to each other.

"Tell me," Krok said. "How do you do it? How?"

"Talent," Stone said. "Sheer talent." Then the Cave Boy winked. "And a little help from my friends."

Notes

* Third position, or Slant Harp, is the style of harmonica playing that sometimes sounds better than Cross Harp when accompanying songs in minor keys.

* The Slant Harp Formlula is to count back two steps from the key the music is in. If the song is in the key of **B** minor, COUNT BACK TWO STEPS (including the **B**) and play an **A** harp.

A B C D E F G
2 1

* When playing Slant Harp, the Notes of Resolution are 1 draw, 4 draw and 8 draw.

* Since Slant Harp is usually played on holes 4 draw and above, it works best on the lower-keyed harps such as **G** and **A**.

ELEVEN

Hubie's Blues or Everything I Almost Forgot to Put in the Book

So ends the saga of Stone, Umm, Krok, Gref and Smash. In Chapter XI, you and the author will meet an unforgettable character, learn some additional information on harp playing, and perhaps come to believe in a strange theory of musical reincarnation.

Hubie's Blues

Do you believe in reincarnation?

I didn't used to. Then I met Hubie. He was down at the bus station, sitting on his suitcase, softly playing the harmonica.

I couldn't hear him too well, so I moved closer. He was playing a Cross Harp style. I recognized some of the riffs. The tone was familiar, too. Still, there was something special about this guy's playing. It had those extra touches of feeling and grace that distinguish a good harpist from a pro.

He looked at me through his dark glasses and said, "Hey, are you that cat, Gindick?"

"All depends," I replied, with a grin, flattered a player this good would know who I am.

"Recognized you by your picture," he said. "Read your book, *Country and Blues Harmonica for the Musically Hopeless*."

"What did you think?" I asked him.

"Good book for beginners. 'Course, no book is going to do it all. A guy or gal can know everything there is to know about the harp, and still not play it with any feeling."

"Unfortunately, you can't teach feeling," I said.

"Yeah, but you can encourage people to use feeling. Everybody's got it. It just comes out of some folks easier than others."

"Look," I said, "I'm writing a new book on harp playing. It's called *Rock n' Blues Harmonica*. I wonder if you'll take a look."

"Sure," he said.

I got into my suitcase and pulled out the tattered manuscript I'd been working on for months. "This is it," I announced, and handed it to him. I wondered if my new book had "feeling."

As he thumbed through the pages, I summarized the book for him. "It starts out telling people about the structure of music. Then it moves into the harmonica, explaining Straight Harp, Cross Harp and Slant Harp. Then it shows a bunch of riffs, how to play riffs in the I-IV-V progression, how to bend notes, how to use your hands . . ."

"Hmmmm," he said. "Looks pretty good, but I think you're leaving out some stuff people might want to know."

"Like what?" I asked, fighting the defensiveness that was creeping into my voice.

"Oh, stuff like using microphones and amps, the difference between using harp as a lead instrument and as a filler, tongue blocking, position playing, good harp players to listen to."

"Guess I could add another chapter," I muttered.

"Yeah, write another chapter and name it after me. Name's Hubie." He held out his hand and we shook.

"I can see it now," he chuckled. "Everything I Forgot to Put in the Book, or Hubie's Blues."

"Great title," I agreed.

"BUS 827 LEAVING IN 20 MINUTES FOR BAKERSFIELD," boomed a voice over the loud speaker.

Hubie looked at his watch. "Don't have much time," he said.

"Well, tell me what to write," I said, pulling out a pen and pad.

"Okay," Hubie said, "let's start with microphones."

Sitting there on his suitcase, Hubie began explaining microphones to me. I wrote as fast as I could, and had some difficulty reading my writing later. Nonetheless, I think I got the gist of it.

189

The Art of Electric Harp

"I like to play country blues, folk blues, country western blues harp," Hubie said, "and in most cases, I play these styles by playing into a vocal mic sitting in a mic stand. But I also love rock and blues, and let's face it, most blues and rock harmonica is *electric* harmonica. Blowing your blues into a raspy-voiced, hand-held mic plugged into a pair of pounding 10-inch speakers, blasting it out like an electric guitar or sax onto some crowded, beer-smellin' dance floor while the band cooks . . . heck . . . that's about as good as it gets.

"Make this a rule: Every person who wants to play electric harmonica has to get the CD, *The Best of Muddy Waters*. The granddaddy of electric harp, Little Walter Jacobs, plays on every cut. Little Walter played in the '40s and '50s, and he pretty much set the standard for *every* blues player who has followed. Get his music into your bones by listening. Listen to Little Walter's tone and the way he plays the riffs. *Listen* to the nuances. *Study* this music with your ears. Why? Because that's your education. Little Walter 101.

"Now, say you're coming along. You've bought a few other keys of harps and you'd like to get that big electric sound. Well, you're gonna have to get yourself a mic and an amp, and learn a few techniques. See, the start of real rock n' blues harp is the handheld microphone. You cup the mic right into the harp and you play in the handcupped position.

"There are two basic kinds of mics that harp players use. The first is the DYNAMIC, which pretty accurately reproduces the sounds that come into it. A lot of great harp players—from Paul Butterfield to James Cotton to John Popper—have used dynamic mics. They're built to pick up the sounds of a variety of musical instruments—

190

everything from violin to guitar to trombone to the human voice singing. You can tell which harp player is using the dynamic because these mics are usually ball-ended.

"The second type is shaped more like a bullet. It's called a CRYSTAL or BULLET mic. This is an old-fashioned mic originally used in broadcasting in the '30s and '40s. These mics (which break if you drop them) were designed to cut through static, crowd noise etc. Frankly, they have pretty lousy fidelity. But, as the great blues players from the '40s and '50s discovered, they make a well-played blues harp sound great. These days crystal mics are made expressly for harp players. The best ones—and most difficult to use—are the Astatic, the Green Bullet, the BluesBlaster.

"But there are also guys who are inventing new mics, like Shaky Joe Harless out of Arizona. This cat makes the SHAKER—a smaller, easier-to-use mic with a built-in volume control and a sound as deep and rich as Southern molasses.

"You can also scour garage sales for a truly old mic, and maybe buy it for a song. You can get some really wicked old stuff. That $5 dictaphone mic you bought from your next-door neighbor might be the best blues mic yet (or worst). Get adapters from Radio Shack and you'll be able to make all the connections.

"Now, you can plug your mic, be it old, new, crystal or dynamic, into lots of weird places. Most harp players agree electric harp sounds best played through a tube amplifier. Hard core blues guys get the FENDER TWIN REVERB BASSMAN or another tube driven amp of the same ilk. These antique guitar amps are what harp players used in the '50s. They get incredible deep, rich, warm sound with the handheld mic. Problem is, you have to turn these behemoth tube amps up really loud to get their benefits.

"Beginners will do fine with a smaller, less expensive PRACTICE AMP (usually solid state). Important features are 'GAIN' and 'VOL-UME' so you can get distortion, 'REVERBERATION' for a echo, and a line-out so you can plug your amp into the P.A. when performing with a band. You can get real portable with the battery-operated PIGNOSE AMP. Or, get your yourself a ROCKMAN, which is the size of a Walkman radio and plays through headphones.

Getting Great Amplified Tone

"So let's assume you have an amplifier and a mic. To get started, try to form a airtight cup with your hands that includes the mic and the harp. Bring this gourd of flesh and metal to your face, and lay the sides of your thumbs on your cheekbones to make a complete enclosure. That's how you hold the mic and harp.

"About plugging in . . . first, turn the volume all the way down! As you softly play a 2 draw or 6 blow, slowly turn the volume up until you can hear yourself through the speaker.

"Now let's set the levels of the bass, treble, gain and volume. As a prelude to what I'm going to say: rule of thumb, for harmonica, emphasize the bass and midrange. Turn the high frequency or treble sounds down. The idea is to get as much "body" as you possibly can. Go for the meat of the note, that sweet spot that makes it so rich.

"Almost all amps have separate 'gain' and 'volume' controls. The higher you turn the 'gain' up and the 'volume' down, the more distortion is produced. DISTORTION (with a hint of reverb) is the essence of that electric sound. It's gritty and modern and makes the harp as powerful as any other instrument on the stage. Think of it as the gonads of electric harp (can you say that in a harp book?). At first, everyone uses as much distortion as they can get, but eventually they back off into a clearer more pleasing, slightly distorted tone.

"Now let's talk REVERBERATION and the part it plays in great electric harp. Reverberation gives the harp an echo—and what could be better than that? So use it! Problem is: if you use too much reverb, your harp tone gets tinny and nonsubstantial." He tapped his ear. "You have to listen. *Really* listen and experiment. The main rule is this: never use so much effect that what your listeners hear is the effect, rather than the harp.

"I also think your readers should know about special effects such as DIGITAL DELAY—which produces incredible echo effects on demand and OVERDRIVE—which allows you amazing distortion

192

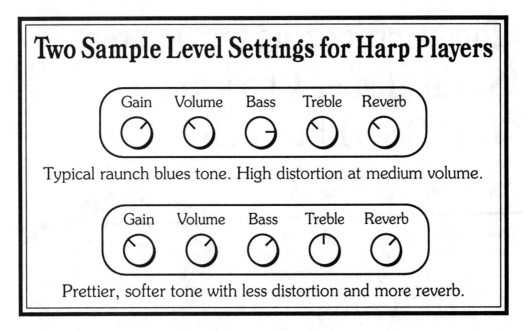

Two Sample Level Settings for Harp Players

Gain   Volume   Bass   Treble   Reverb

Typical raunch blues tone. High distortion at medium volume.

Gain   Volume   Bass   Treble   Reverb

Prettier, softer tone with less distortion and more reverb.

without having to tweak your amp. These electronic boxes are staples for electric guitar players and can be equally important in good electric harp. If you're in search of greater variety in your sound, these may be the answer, especially if your amp isn't the best.

"Now that the levels are set, back away from the amplifier (maybe turn it up a little bit first!) and assume that fully handcupped position with harp and mic. Getting feedback or warnings of it? Get rid of it by doing any of these things:

1. Move mic away from speaker's direction.
2. Turn treble or higher frequencies down.
3. Turn down the volume.

"Concentrate, and play a long, well-puckered 3 blow or 2 draw. If your hands form an airtight seal between mic and harp, and if your volume's sufficient,that note no longer sounds like a harmonica. Instead, it's more horn-like, or sounds like a fuzzed-out electric guitar. Try it on a wailing 4 draw. Bend that note down and bring it up. Don't be afraid of your sound, rather, milk it! Remember: GRITTY IS GOOD.

Hubie got up off his suitcase, and looked down the road. "Think that bus is late." Suddenly a harp appeared in his hand and he began to play a lonesome waiting-for-the-bus blues.

Tongue-Blocking for Octaves, Sophisticated Chords and That Deep Blues Pulse

This guy was good. Along with his riveting single notes, he kept coming back to this one technique — a sound like a bluesy accordian, separate notes warbling at the same time. It was uncanny. I finally stopped him. "What are you doing?"

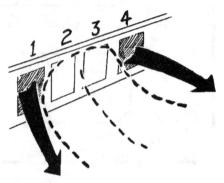

"Tongue-blocking octaves," said Hubie. "Draw 1234, and use your tongue to cover holes 23. The result is 1 and 4 draw playing at the same time: octaves. On your **C** harp, it's a funky **D** chord. This the old-fashioned way of playing harp, but it's coming back into style— especially among amplified blues players.

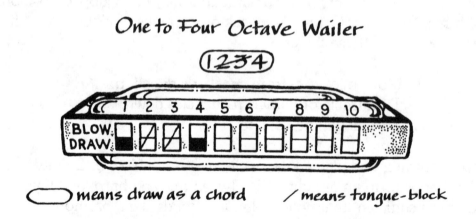

One to Four Octave Wailer

(1234)

⬯ means draw as a chord   / means tongue-block

"Because it plays out Wailing Notes 1 and 4 at the same time, the 1 to 4 Octave Wailer is exactly that. It expresses the V chord. It creates tension . . . and is a very interesting sound. Subtle changes in the placement of your tongue easily change this sound. For instance, as soon as I lift my tongue so 23 draw are also playing, I've got the Cross Harp Chord of Resolution, 1234 draw.

Tongue-Blocking Combinations and Cycles for Second Position

"The great thing about tongue-blocking octaves is that you can move your embouchure all over the harmonica and get tones with important musical values. It is fairly easy to go from single notes to octaves to chords and back."

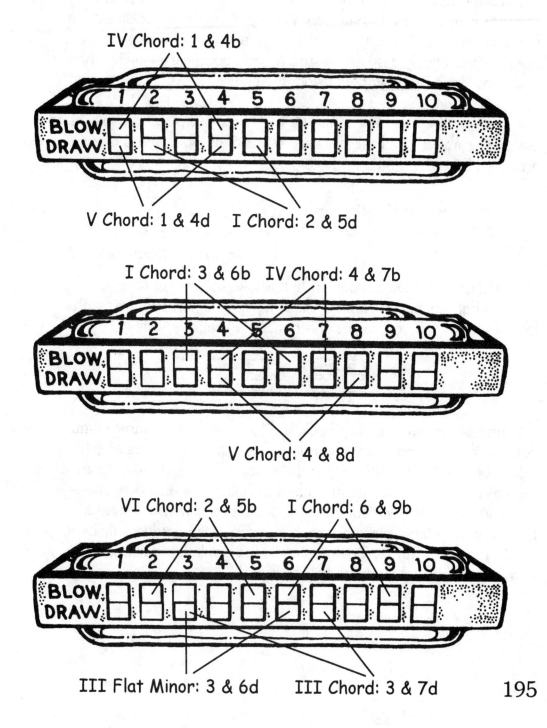

IV Chord: 1 & 4b

V Chord: 1 & 4d   I Chord: 2 & 5d

I Chord: 3 & 6b   IV Chord: 4 & 7b

V Chord: 4 & 8d

VI Chord: 2 & 5b   I Chord: 6 & 9b

III Flat Minor: 3 & 6d   III Chord: 3 & 7d

195

And Don't Forget the Headshake!

Wailing on the 4 draw, Hubie started moving his harp back and forth across his lips. The result was a startling two-note cavalcade of hipness that made the hairs on the back of my neck stand at attention and dance.

"That's the headshake," Hubie said. "All you have to do is slide the harp (or move your lips) between 4 and 5 draw very quickly as you get a single note. It's like using the same airstream on two different notes. It's relatively easy and it sure sounds good—especially when you bend the note down and bring it back up.

"You can do the headshake all over the harp, but playing Cross Harp diatonic, some of the best ideas are 4 and 5 draw, 2 and 3 draw, and 3 and 4 draw, and 5 and 6 blow.

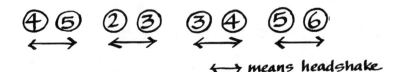

⟷ means headshake

"In addition to bending, you can headshake as you get tongue-blocked-octaves and chromatic harp harmonies. Amplify this with lots of reverb and you've got another Little Walter specialty.

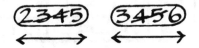

"When I say 'move the harp back and forth,' I don't mean to limit you. Some guys move it up and down very quickly, others side to side, others slant it. The point is the single note headshake is one of the easiest of all the techniques I'm describing. It's also versatile—working for blues, rock and country. It's an easy way to sound as though you've been playing for years, even when you've only been playing for days, and will get any audience applauding almost immediately. So tell your readers to use it!"

196

<u>D</u> Blues on the <u>C</u> Chromatic

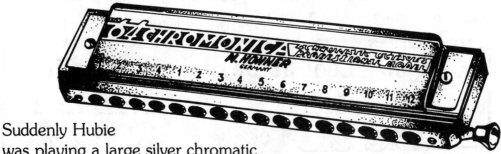

Suddenly Hubie
was playing a large silver chromatic
harmonica and, man, did it sound good.

I had fooled around with a chromatic, had learned a few songs, but
when it came to jamming I always got lost with the slide, not knowing when to press it in or let it out. I also couldn't bend notes on the
crazy thing—which has always seemed like a prerequisite for the
blues.

But now, Hubie was making his chromatic sound bluesy, even jazzy,
with big tone, big chords, no bends—that Little Walter sound. I
pulled my '64 Chro' from my harp bag. It felt big and intimidating in
my hand as Hubie quit playing and started to teach.

"Now the chro' is usually overlooked by people who already play the
10-hole diatonic because it's bigger, and because they can't figure
out the slide." Hubie shook his head. "This is a real shame because
the chromatic harmonica is a monster, and, as a lot of great
bluesmen prove, all you have to do with the slide is: IGNORE IT.
That's right, stop fiddlin' around with the damned thing. Now the
instrument is a lot simpler."

This made me laugh. I always thought I'd have to *master* the slide.
Instead, to play the blues, I could *forget* about it.

"What we do is play this instrument 3rd Position Slant Harp style,
emphasizing the draw chords and the draw notes. By
emphasizing the draw notes, you get an automatic blues/jazz scale in
the key of **D.** Or, you can press the slide in, and keep it in, and
play in the key of **E** flat. Either way, Notes of Resolution are 1 draw
(both bass and midrange), 5 draw and 9 draw. And, avoid 4 draw
like the plague, because it's a Clash Note!

"On the chro' 64 (my favorite), the first four holes are bass notes. These are exactly the same as holes 5 through 8, only an octave lower. Skip over them for now and go to the fifth hole where the numbers start again and go up to 12.

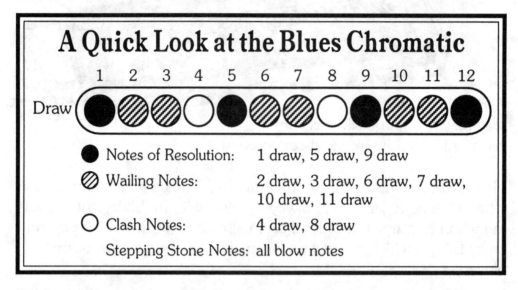

"The midrange 1 draw (the D note) is a good place to start. The basic idea is to take draw/blow patterns up and down your harp, always skipping over 4 draw and 8 draw because they're not part of the scale resolving on 1 draw or 5 draw or 9 draw. Some chromatic riffs are . . ." And he began to play a sweet chromatic harp blues.

Positions 1 Through 6 Plus 12
Playing Harp in Seven Different Keys

Hubie was on a roll. "You've talked about 1st position Straight Harp, 2nd position Cross Harp, 3rd position Slant Harp. I'm going to show you 4th, 5th, 6th and 12th positions. They're not that hard."

"Do me a favor. Define 'position.'" I said. "Folks get confused."

Hubie thought for a moment. "Although the **C** harp was originally intended to be played in the key of **C**, you can play in different keys by choosing a different Note of Resolution. Because the harmonica has missing notes, you get different scales, modes and musical feelings.

"When I play **C** harp to music in the key of **C**, using 1 blow, 4 blow, 7 blow and 10 blow for my Notes of Resolution, I'm playing 1st position Straight Harp.

1st Position Notes of Resolution (C harp key of C)

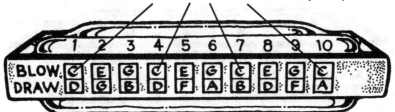

1st Position Up and Down Riff

4   5   ⑤   6   6   ⑤   5   4

"The next position folks learn is 2nd or Cross Harp. Here we play the **C** harmonica in the key of **G**. Exploring the difference between the 1st position "Red River Valley" on page 55 and the 2nd position version on page 160 as well as the two versions of "Saints" on page 167 gives you a good idea of how positions work. Same song, same harp, but what a difference. First position sounds as though the song was written by Stephen Foster. Second position sounds as though the song was written by Little Walter."

"As I just mentioned, playing 2nd Position Cross Harp, you play your **C** harp in the key of **G**–using 2 draw, 3 blow, 6 blow and 9 blow, 2-5 draw and 3-6 blow tongue-blocks and the 1234 draw chord as your Notes of Resolution. As noted, 2nd position gives a blues twinge to your music. And that's why 90% of contemporary harping is in 2nd.

2nd Position Notes of Resolution (C harp key of G)

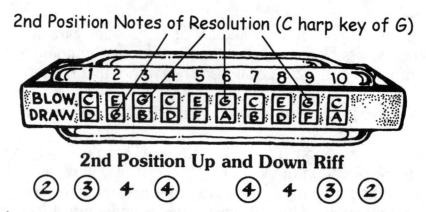

2nd Position Up and Down Riff

② ③ 4 ④   ④ 4 ③ ②

"For 3rd position or Slant Harp, resolve your riffs and songs on the **C** harp's **D** notes, using 1 draw, 4 draw, 8 draw and the tongue blocks at 1-4 draw and 4-8 draw. The 3rd position version of 'Joshua' on page 162 and 'House of the Rising Sun' gets you playing in minor keys.

3rd Position Notes of Resolution (C harp in D minor)

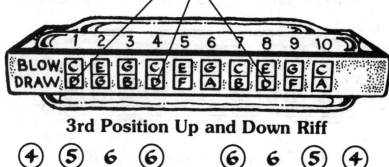

3rd Position Up and Down Riff

④ ⑤ 6 ⑥   ⑥ 6 ⑤ ④

"First, 2nd and 3rd positions are three distinctly different modes on one harp. The term 'mode' refers to 'Church Mode.' Traveling monks in old Greece used to carry diatonic keyboards with only white keys–much like a harmonica. By starting and ending their songs on keys other than the **C** note they derived different styles of music. Translated to harp, 1st position is the **Ionic Mode**. Second position is the **Mixolydian Mode**. Third position is the **Dorian Mode**.

"Each time you change positions you count 5 steps up the musical scale. Just as **G** is the 5th note of the **C** scale, **D** is the 5th note of the **G** scale. What's the 5th note of the **D** scale? **A**, which is 4th position. Knowing this won't necessarily help you play, but it sure sounds impressive, especially when you talk to those conservatory cats."

Fourth Position Minor Key Music

"In 4th position, you play **C** harp in the key of **A** minor. The **A** notes are at 3 draw**, 6 draw and 10 draw. The feeling is Eastern European, or Gypsy, and this is called the **Aeolian Mode**. Beginning and ending songs on 3 draw** can be awkward, but playing the 4th position 'Joshua' on page 162 will help you learn, or at least appreciate the challenge. You also get the opportunity to distinguish between the 3 draw bent and the 3 draw unbent. Truth be told, it's easier to use riffs that resolve on the 6 draw, but man, you need those low notes."

4th Position Notes of Resolution (C harp, key of A minor)

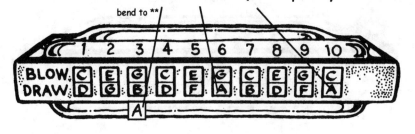

4th Position Up and Down Riff

③** ③ 4 ④ 5   5 ④ 4 ③ ③**

4th Position Octave Scale Up

③** ③ 4 ④ 5 ⑤ 6 ⑥

4th Position Octave Scale Down

⑥ 6 ⑤ 5 ④ 4 ③ ③**

4th Position High Octave Scale Up

⑥ ⑦ 7 ⑧ 8 ⑨ 9 ⑩

4th Position 6 Draw Wailing Resolver

⑥ 6 5 ⑥

Fifth Position Minor Key Music

"Let's go on to 5th position," Hubie said. "Here you play your **C** harp in the key of **E** minor. The **E** notes on your **C** harp are at 2 blow, 5 blow and 8 blow, and you can tongue-block octaves at the 2-5 blow and the 5-8 blow. The music you get up here is minor key jazz blues, reminiscent of Tom Waits, Ray Charles, Louis Prima or even Cab Calloway. The classical Greek name is the **Phrygian Mode**. It has a Middle Eastern flavor–particularly if you use the 2 draw bent as well as the 2 draw unbent. A great thing about this position is that bending isn't necessary. It just adds.

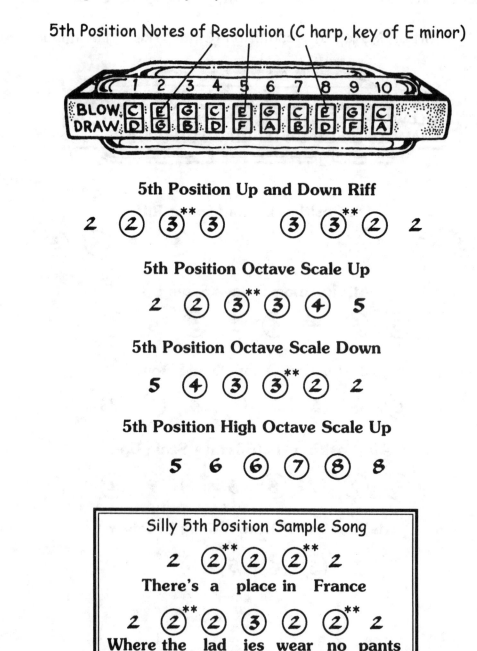

5th Position Notes of Resolution (C harp, key of E minor)

5th Position Up and Down Riff

2　②　③**　③　　③　③**　②　2

5th Position Octave Scale Up

2　②　③**　③　④　5

5th Position Octave Scale Down

5　④　③　③**　②　2

5th Position High Octave Scale Up

5　6　⑥　⑦　⑧　8

Silly 5th Position Sample Song

2　②**　②　②**　2
There's　a　place in　France

2　②**　②　③　②　②**　2
Where the　lad　ies　wear　no　pants

202

Sixth Position Minor Key Music

"Sixth is the most esoteric of the positions I play. It's your **C** harp in **B** minor, but what a weird **B** minor. The Notes of Resolution are at 3 draw unbent, 7 draw and 3-7 draw tongue-blocked octave. To me, it's like big band blues." Hubie gave me a wide-eyed-blow-your-mind type of look and started playing. Out came a totally new harmonica sound, like a wild hornblast from the trumpet of Harry James.

6th Position Notes of Resolution (C harp, key of B minor)

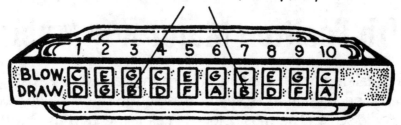

6th Position Up and Down Riff

③ ④ 5 ⑤   ⑤ 5 ④ ③

"It's that 5 draw Wailing Note that gives it such a big band feeling," he said. "I love whipping out my **C** harp when a guy is playing in the key of **B** minor or **B** minor 7th. Your guitarist won't believe what he's hearing. And I mean that in the good sense."

6th Position Octave Scale Up

③ ④ 5 ⑤ ⑥ ⑦

6th Position High Up and Down

⑦ ⑧ 8 ⑨ 8 ⑧ ⑦

"Feel free to bend the 3 draw before playing the 3 draw unbent. The 3 draw bent is the flatted 7th and adds a nice touch. Here's a cool riff."

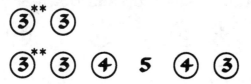

③** ③

③** ③ ④ 5 ④ ③

Positions 7 through 11

"Positions 7 through 11 might be more theoretical than actual because they have to be played almost entirely on bent notes (though there are guys who do it). 7th position is in **F** sharp. 8th position is in **D** flat. 9th position is in **A** flat. 10th position is in **E** flat. 11th position is in **B** flat. Most folks get to these keys by pulling out a harp that's in a flatted key, and playing positions out of that.

Twelfth Position Major Key Music

"Now we're talking about playing **C** harp in the key of **F**, using 5 draw, 2 draw bent and 9 draw as Notes of Resolution. It's a bluesy way to play a melodic scale. The musicologists call it the **Lydian Mode**. I don't know who Lydia was, but judging by the music, she was smart, fun and pretty darn easy to be around."

12th Position Notes of Resolution (C harp, key of F)

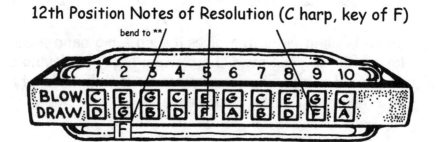

"'Amazing Grace' on page 163 is an excellent example of how 12th position works. Instead of 5 draw, the song starts on 4 blow. Usually, 12th position works best on songs that start on the 5th note of the scale, like 'Amazing Grace.' This is kind of like your Good Morning Riff, only more melodic. Below, start the scale on the 4 blow, as though you were playing 1st position. If you leave out the 5 blow, and remember your Note of Resolution is actually 5 draw, you'll be playing in the key of **F**, adding a new musical style to your repertoire.

12th Position Up and Down Scale

4 ④ ⑤ 6 ⑥ 7 ⑧ ⑨

⑨ ⑧ 7 ⑥ 6 ⑤

Practical Position Playing

"Many harp players who are accomplished at 1st and 2nd positions are intimidated by 3rd, 4th, 5th, 6th and 12th," Hubie said. "What they may not realize is that learning 2nd position gives them all the skills they need. The problem is often in *hearing* the music in the position. That's where learning songs like 'Joshua' and 'Amazing Grace' come in. They direct the ear as the player tries to fathom how this unfamiliar sequence of notes can lead to music.

"Learning new positions helps in many ways. One is that your playing can now be better suited to the music you are accompanying. There is a huge difference between 12th, 2nd and 1st positions, yet they can all play the same material. Choose the voice that best suits the song, and you. Not everything has to sound like blues. Not everything should.

"Another big advantage is that you can often adjust to key changes within a song without having to pick up a different key of harp. You can play 'chordally.' If you know a song is moving from a **G** chord into, say, an **E** minor chord, you can quickly switch from 2nd to 5th positions then back to 2nd when the song returns to a **G** chord. Usually we just fashion scales to meet the song's chord progression. Playing 'chordally' is an alternative way of thinking about the harp.

"And lastly, playing positions makes it all more fun."

This I could believe, for Hubie looked to me like a happy man.

To Play in Key of	Use These Harps for These Positions						
	1st	2nd	3rd	4th	5th	6th	12th
C	C	F	B♭	E♭	A♭	D♭	G
D	D	G	C	F	B♭	E♭	A
E	E	A	D	G	C	F	B
F	F	B♭	E♭	A♭	D♭	F#	C
G	G	C	F	B♭	E♭	A♭	D
A	A	D	G	C	F	B♭	E
B	B	E	A	D	G	C	F#
Notes of Reso- lution	1 blow 4 blow 7 blow 10 blow	2 draw 3 blow 6 blow 9 blow	1 draw 4 draw 8 draw	3 draw bent 6 draw 10 draw	2 blow 5 blow 8 blow	3 draw 7 draw	2 draw bent 5 draw 9 draw
				Work best when music is in a minor key			

205

Playing the Diatonic Harp as a Chromatic Instrument

"If you can hear it in your mind, you can do it on the harp," Hubie suddenly said. "Potentially, you can play your little diatonic harp in all twelve keys. You'd bend your way into a chromatic scale instead of the eight toned scale that the diatonic harp was made for, and then play riffs or scales that resolve out of each of these twelve tones."

"Sounds impossible," I muttered.

"Thing is, you have to think chromatically for this to happen and keep exploring that harp past the limitations. Getting to be a harp player is an inner thing, and guys with chromatic minds have turned the harp into a chromatic instrument.

"Some guys get a chromatic scale out of a diatonic harp by putting windsavers over the reeds. These little pieces of plastic make bending a lot easier, though some people say they change the tone.

"Other guys use a technique called the **overblow**. The 5 blow overblow gives you a tone halfway between the 5 draw and 6 blow, and the 6 blow overblow gives you a tone between the 6 draw and the 7 draw. This was made famous by a very fine gentleman and musical genius called **Howard Levy**. Howard is a jazz pianist who decided he wanted to play chromatic jazz on the diatonic harp. He discovered a way of bending those blow notes up, and revolutionized the way advanced harp players think about their instruments.

"Nowadays, 2nd position is a jumping off place for learning to play fluently in as many different positions as possible, and finally, being able to play the diatonic harmonica as though it were a chromatic instrument that has all 12 tones, sharps and flats. When you reach that point, you're no longer playing positions. You're playing chromatic harmonica on a diatonic instrument." His eyes took on that special Hubie gleam. "Now that's a worthy goal in my estimation.

206

"On the other hand, what's important here is making music, not the number of positions you can play, or the number of bends you can achieve. As a guy I know said, 'If you can play three and a half positions, you're good.'"

"Sure, sure," I said. "Show me this overblow."

Overblowing, Overdrawing— Over the Top

Hubie pulled out a dented, old beater harp and quickly unscrewed the top plate. "Listen," he said and blew into hole five as he crimped the reed with his finger. The note swung upward and Hubie was suddenly playing a much higher note. "That's it," he said, "That's the overblow, a step and a half higher than the five.

"The trick is to get the reed next door to the one you're playing going in the opposite direction. Overblowing 5 blow, I slightly block-off the air going into the hole in such a way that . . . get this . . . the 5 draw starts playing a half step up."

"Come on," I protested.

"No, that's exactly what happens." He handed the reed plate to me. I used my fingernail to touch the top reed near its base, and, sure enough, as I blew, that note squealed upward with a tone not unlike one of those confetti-dangling, party horns.

"Whoa!"

"The idea now, " Hubie said, "is to figure out a way to get this effect without touching the reed with your finger. Some guys accomplish it by bending 6 draw as far down as they can and then blowing, keeping the mouth in the same position. A successful result is the 6 blow overblow, a **B flat** on your **C** harp, same note as 3 draw half-step bend, but up an ocatave."

"Other guys describe that overblow motion as being a little bit like coughing on a blow bend.

"Another technique is you open up your harp, and carefully measure and close the gap on the reeds. This takes lots of experimentation and the proper tools, but man, when you're closing in on an overblow, a little open harp surgery can be just what the doctor ordered. Let me give you an idea of how a complete chromatic scale goes."

The Chromatic Scale on a Diatonic "C" Harp

C	D♭	D	E♭	E	F	F#	G	A♭	A	B♭	B
1	①*	①	1o	2	②**	②*	②	③***	③**	③*	③

C	D♭	D	E♭	E	F	F#	G	A♭	A	B♭	B
4	④*	④	4o	5	⑤	5o	6	⑥*	⑥	6o	⑦

C	D♭	D	E♭	E	F	F#	G	A♭	A	B♭	B	C	D♭
7	⑦o	⑧	8*	8	⑨	9*	9	⑨o	⑩	10**	10*	10	10o

        * 1/2 step bend
     ** 1 step bend
  *** 1-1/2 step bend
     o overblow or overdraw

I was trying my overblow on the 6 blow and it just wasn't coming. "Don't *try* to overblow," he said. "Try to stop the normal flow of air so the overblow can happen. You need a blocked feeling—and you use your mouth, throat, tongue and air pressure to get it. That blocked feeling is what makes the opposite reed vibrate."

I kept trying it with small result— only a series of blurps, wholps, screeches and blats from this instrument I thought (before today) I had mastered. Finally, Hubie took pity on me. "Don't get too frustrated. This is a project that'll take a guy years." He looked at his harp happily. "It's nice to have something to look forward to."

Open Harp Surgery–
Fixing the Sticky Harp

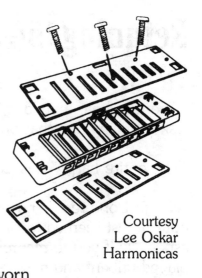

Courtesy
Lee Oskar
Harmonicas

"The reeds on these little harps are like little girlfriends," Hubie said. "They require maintenance and tune-ups. If you let it go too long, you might as well throw'm away. Treat 'em right, and they'll treat you right. That's why it's a good idea for every serious harp player to carry one of these." From his worn gig bag, he produced a small guitar tuner and black-cased tool kit embossed with the words "Lee Oskar Harmonica Tuning System."

"What we have here are some jewelers' files, an automotive feeler gauge and Phillips-head screwdriver. You can get these tools at any hardware store, but Lee puts it all together with an instruction booklet.

"One of the first things to remember about repairing your harp is that the draw reeds are on the bottom of your harp and on the outside of your reed-plate. The blow reeds are on the top, inside the harp.

"If you don't want to deal with repairing reeds, and also don't want to buy a new harp, you can use new reed-plates. Both Hohner and Lee Oskar sell these, and they make a lot of sense. Still, there are repairs that will keep you from having to buy new reed-plates. One of these is adjusting the **gap** to fix a sticky harp "

"Say, in the course of playing, you go for a note, maybe a 4 draw and it just won't play. The problem may be in your technique, might be gunk in the reeds, or it may be the space between the reed and the reed-plate.

"A real tight gap or space makes the harp stick, and a wide gap makes the harp play too airily. Take the covers off and use the feeler gauge or even a razor blade to slightly push the draw reed away from the reed-plate, or to push it slightly back in. The reed is fragile, but not incredibly so." He plucked it to make his point. "The main thing is to maintain the natural upward curve of the reed.

"If the problem is a blow reed, you can widen the gap by pushing the upper reed down into the harp. If you need to close the gap, you'll need to take the reed-plate off and then narrow the gap."

209

Retuning the Harp

"I went to hear a buddy play." Hubie said. "Now, I have the unpleasant task of telling him that on several songs, his harp was out of tune."

"The entire harp?" I asked.

"No, just one reed, and only a little, but every time he crossed that note, it just seemed to clang. If you are playing professionally, and especially if you're recording, check the pitch of your harp's reeds played unbent and make sure you're not wildly out of tune on one reed. Particularly dangerous are blow reeds that might be sharp."

He played a 3 blow at the tuner's built-in mic and I watched the needle dance across the meter. "Because of the harp's natural vibrato, needles on these gauges jump all over the place. Even with the tuner, you're doing it somewhat by ear. I try to play each reed unbent, as high as I possibly can."

He held the reed-plate to the pallid light that filtered through the filthy bus station windows. "If you want to tune the reed so it produces a higher pitch, file, scrape or shave the free end of the reed (with a shim underneath to give support). If you want to tune downward, file the base of the reed. This makes it vibrate slower, lowering the pitch.

File fixed end to lower pitch

File free end to raise pitch

"Use the tuner to reference your tuning. You can either pluck the reed with the feeler gauge, or you can keep putting your harp back together (without the screws) and blowing or drawing, so you can file and listen, file and listen until the needle on the guitar tuner behaves, and you sound as though you're in tune. Expect to ruin a few harps while you learn. Some pros tune every harp they play, even new ones out of the box, even new reed-plates. Other guys, and I'm talking about fine players, just throw the clunkers away and break out a new harp.

Tuning kit and booklet highly recommended.
Count on ruining the first few harps you experiment on.
Do not skimp on quality of guitar tuner. Be delicate!

Using Music Notation

"Now comes the dreaded topic," said Hubie. "I realize a lot of harp players are sensitive because they don't read music. One reason is that it seems not directly applicable to the harp in any key other than **C**. To rely on music reading, and have to calculate how the note-location changes every time you play a song written for **D**, or **F**, and have to pick up another harp, would require a doctorate in music (or at last a very smart guy).

"'It's not what the harp's all about,' is what most guys think. Well, I kind of agree with that. Anything that reminds me of my 6th grade trombone teacher is enough to send me packing, harp or no harp."

"You played trombone, too?" I asked in amazement.

He looked at me with those crinkly eyes. "If you want to get better as a harp player, reading standard notation, even if only for the key of **C**, will be a great help. Entire worlds of music will open up to you. Following along with how some guy wrote a concerto 200 years ago will give you a whole new way to connect the dots. There isn't much blues harp notation, but there is some. And it's not really that hard. My problem is that I can't keep myself from improvising each time I start to read. That's just the way the harp is.

"Like guitar music, harp music is usually written on the treble clef, up one octave from where it actually sounds out. Let me write out a basic staff for the **C** harp." And so he did.

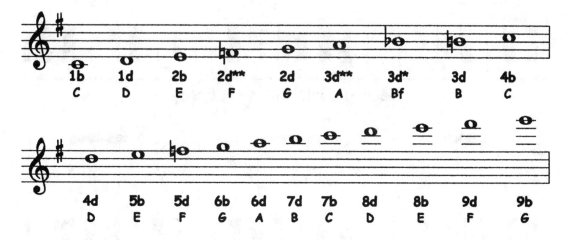

211

Pick Up Some Basic Guitar and Piano Knowledge

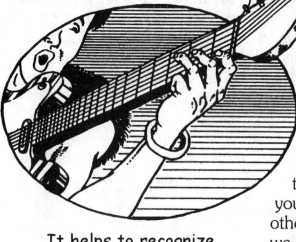

It helps to recognize chords and chord changes!

After awhile, Hubie suggested it might be cooler in the bar. We sat next to an old upright. "Anyone interested in the musical theory part of the harp would do well to take a few piano lessons. Because the harp is tucked away inside your mouth and is so different from other mainstream instruments, we harp players get no visual feedback. Tying the harp to a piano in your mind isn't a bad idea.

He opened his battered guitar case and pulled out a beat-up old guitar. "I also think a harp player needs to know some basic guitar chords, just so he can recognize the progressions from watching the guitar player's hands. It also helps not having to ask what key the music is in." He then walked me through some chords in the I-IV-V progression.

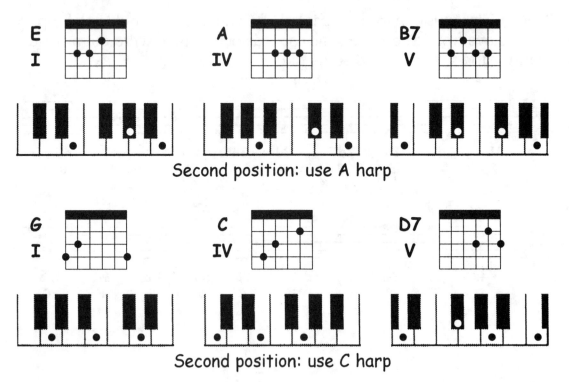

212

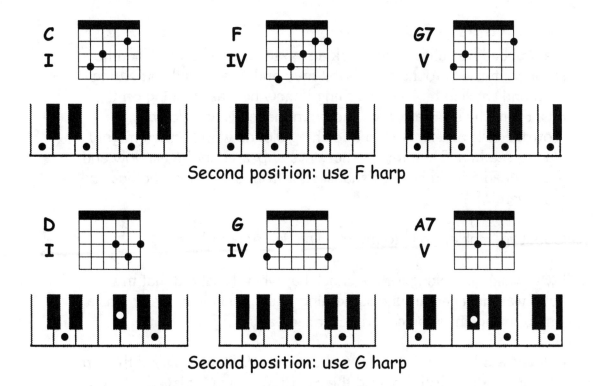

Second position: use F harp

Second position: use G harp

Watching Hubie comfortably expressing himself in the world of music filled me with exhilaration. This was what I wanted. I wanted music! More music! I resolved right then and there to become a terrific harp player. *Really* terrific! I wanted to be the best.

The Magic Harmonica

Suddenly a silver bus turned up the street and came noisily into the terminal. You could smell the exhaust and the grime of the road. Somehow, the harmonica fit this scene perfectly. People were scurrying around the bus station, lugging suitcases, saying their goodbyes.

Hubie gave me a grin. "Well, I gotta go..."

"Play something first," I said. "Just a lick. I'd like to hear you once more."

Hubie looked at the bus's open door, pulled out his harp and cupped it in his hands. *Waaaaa!* the harp moaned. *Waaaaa! Taa Waa Wa!*

Lord, it was sweet!

"And that," he said, "is Hubie's Blues."

213

He grabbed his suitcase and took a step toward the door. Then he stopped, turned around and shook my hand. He placed something hard and small in it. The next thing I knew he was climbing on the bus. From the sidewalk, I watched him make his way down the crowded aisle and sit next to a fetching blonde who seemed mighty glad to see him. Then three other guys appeared in the window and they all had a good laugh. Exhaust shot from the rear of the bus and they were off.

Goodbye, Hubie, I said to myself. Thanks for your help.

I was walking, looking for the snack bar when I realized that my hand was clenched around something Hubie had given me. It was a small, strange harmonica. I'd never seen anything like it.

I played a 3 blow, a 4 draw, a 6 draw and a 9 blow. I played the Up and Down Blues Riff, I played the Six Blow Down. I played a Good Morning Riff, I played the Good Morning Riff up to 3 draw, then 3 draw bent down. I couldn't stop playing!

Then I started bending. Low, throaty, growling bends. High soaring bends. Overblows, overdraws, playing positions, playing chromatic! The tone of this harmonica was incredible. It dripped like molasses, it soared like a rocket, it honked like a horn, it sang like a Streisand.

People were looking at me as my harp playing peaked on the bending 10 blow and tumbled through space, over the notes to the 2 draw. Some folks were smiling, tapping their feet. Others had disapproval on their faces.

Finally, I managed to wrestle the harmonica away from my lips. I looked at the harmonica more closely. Yes, this was it. This was the harmonica I'd been looking for all my life.

It was carefully carved from the tusk of a wild boar, and I felt sure that the reeds were from the hard bark of the boo boo tree.

214

Harp-Player's Resource & Music Index

The next few pages tell you what key harmonica you need to jam Cross Harp on each song with some wonderful CDs. How does it work? Put a CD in the player, find the right key of harp for the song you want to play and begin molding harmonica sounds to the sounds of recorded music. Start with your Wailing Notes. Create tension until the music demands resolution.

Cross Harp

Blues Brothers
Briefcase
Full of Blues
Harp: Dan Ackroyd

Can't Turn	F
Bartender	F
Messin'	E
Almost	A
Biscuit	B flat
Shot Gun	E flat
Groove Me	D
Don't Know	C
Soul Man	B flat
B Movie	A
Flip Flop	E flat
Turn You	F

Blues Traveler
Four
Harp: John Popper

Runaround	C
Stand	A flat/D
Look Around	C
Fallible	B
Mountains Win	C/D
Freedom	G
Crash Burn	D
Price to Pay	A
Hook	D
Good, Bad, Ugly	A/D/E
Just Wait	F
Brother John	A/C

Norton Buffalo
Lovin' in the
Valley of the Moon
Harp: Norton Buffalo

Lovin'	C
One Kiss	C
Ghetto	D flat
Nobody	A
Puerto	A
Hangin'	G
Another	B flat
Rosalie	B flat
Jig's Up	D
Eighteen	A
Sea	F

Jimmy Buffett
Changes in Latitudes
Harp: "Fingers" Taylor

Changes	G
Wonder	C
Banana	C
Tampico	D
Lovely	F
Margaritaville	G
Shelter	A
Miss You	F
Biloxi	D
Landfall	C

Paul Butterfield
East Meets West
Harp: Paul Butterfield

Walking Blues	D
Get Out	F
Gotta Mind	F
All These Blues	D
Work Blues	B flat
Mary Mary	D
Two Trains	B flat
Never Say No	B flat
East West	G

Eric Clapton
From the Cradle
Harp: Jerry Portnoy

Blues Before	F sharp
3rd Degree	G
Reconsider	C
Hoochie	D
Five Long	D
Tore Down	F
How Long	A
Going Away	D
Blues Leave	A
Sinners	A
Motherless	E
Hurts Me	F sharp
Someday	G
Standing	B flat
Driftin'	A
Groanin'	D

James Cotton
High Compression
Harp: James Cotton

Potato	E
Yin	F
23 Hours	G*
Doggin'	C
Cuttin'	C
Doin' Bad	A
Sunny	D
Super Harp	F
EZ	C
Compression	C

*Although listing is for cross harp, James plays C chromatic in key of D.

Bob Dylan
Blonde on Blonde
Harp: Bob Dylan

Rainy Day	A
Pledging	D
Visions	D
Sooner or Later	B flat
Your Way	C
Achilles	C
Sweet Marie	G
I Want You	B flat
Memphis Blues	A
Pillbox Hat	D
Like a Woman	A
Fourth Time	A
5 Believers	D
Sad Eyed	G

Bob Dylan
Highway 61
Revisited
Harp: Bob Dylan

Rolling Stone	F
Tombstone	F
Train	D flat
Buick 6	F
Thin Man	G
Queen Jane	F
Highway 61	E flat
Tom Thumb	C
Desolation Row	A

The J. Geils Band
Best of the J. Geils Band
Harp: Magic Dick

Southside	C
Give It	C
Where Did	D
House Party	A
Detroit	F
Whammer	A
I Do	C
Must Got	F
Looking	F

Slim Harpo
The Best of Slim Harpo
Harp: Slim Harpo

Mohair Slim	B
Keep What I Got	B
Scratch My Back	B flat
Buzz Me Baby	A
King Bee	B flat
Rainin'	C
Shake	D
Ten-ni-nee	D
Breadmaker	A
Tip On In	A

Walter Horton
Big Walter Horton
Harp: Big Walter

Good Time	C
Christine	C
Lovin'	A
Boy Blue	B flat
Can't Hold	A
Sun	C
Tell Me	A
Mercy	G
That Ain't	A
Temptation	A
Trouble	D

Walter Jacobs
Little Walter
Harp: Little Walter

My Babe	B flat
Hours	B flat
So Fine	A
Last Night	G
Blues Feel	G
Can't Hold	C
Back	B flat
Too Late	B flat
Feeling	D
Teenage	G
Fool	D
Saucer	G
Juke	A
Old World	B flat
Wall	C
Watch Yourself	A
Blue Lights	G*
Tell Mama	C
Gotta Go	D
Shade	A
Too Late	C
Thunderbird	G*
Baby	C
Boom	A

* Walter played chromatic "C" harp in the key of D (1 and 4 draw notes of resolution) on these numbers. The "G" listing is for regular cross harp.

Bob Marley
Natty Dread

Lively Up	G
No Woman	F
Belly Full	F
Rebel	D
So Jah	G
Natty	D
Bend Down	F
Talkin'	D
Revolution	F

John Mayall
Turning Point
Harp: John Mayall

Laws Change	F
Saw Mill	A
Gonna Fight	E
Hard Share	C
California	G
Roxanne	F
Room to Move	F sharp

Charlie McCoy
The Real McCoy
Harp: Charlie McCoy

Today I Started	B
Orange Blossom	F
Only Daddy	A
Jackson	F
Hangin' On	A
Real McCoy	E
Lovin' Her	D
Easy Lovin'	E flat
How Can I	F
Help Me	A
Country Road	F

Willie Nelson
Stardust
Harp: Mickey Raphael

Stardust	C
Georgia	F sharp
Blue Skies	F
All of Me	C
Unchained	C
September Song	D flat
Sunny Side	C
Moonlight	
Get Around	D
Someone	D

Lee Oskar
Before the Rain
Harp: Lee Oskar

Rain	F sharp
Steppin'	D
SF Bay	F sharp
Feelin'	A flat
Words	F
Sing Song	F sharp
Haunted House	F

Cross Harp

Rod Piazza
Harpburn
Harp: Rod Piazza

Rockin' Robin	D
Bad Boy	C
California Boogie	A
Upsetter	A
Tribute	E*
Harpburn	G*
Feelin' Good	E flat
Honey Bee	F*
Cold Chill	A
Dangerous	G*

* Although the key listed is for cross harp, Rod plays chromatic on these numbers.

Bonnie Raitt
Sweet Forgiveness
Harp: Norton Buffalo

Leave Home	G
Runaway	F
Two Lives	B flat
Louise	D
Gamblin'	G
Forgive	E flat
Farewell	E flat
Three	E
Time	E
Home	A

Jimmy Reed
Upside Your Head
Harp: Jimmy Reed

Shame Shame	A
Baby	A
Ain't Got	A
Ain't Lovin'	B flat
Road	A
Bright Lights	D
Too Much	A
Big Boss Man	A
Upside	D
Good Lover	B flat
Honest	D
Virginia	D
Hush	C
Found Love	D
Baby What	A
Goin' NY	D

Madcat Ruth
Gone Solo
Harp: Madcat Ruth

Sweet Chicago	A
Changed	C
Bad Luck	E flat
Catfish	A
Fishin'	F
Shortnin'	F/G/A
Boom Jake	A
Too Late	C
St. James	F*
Help Me	D*
Hurts Me	C
Nobody	G*
Sonny Terry	D
Rollin'	D

*On St. James, Madcat plays F sharp in 5th position (2 blow note of resolution), In Help Me, he plays D harp in 3rd position (slant harp, 4 draw note of resolution). On Nobody, he plays G harp in 12th position (5 draw note of resolution).

George Smith
Oopin' Doopin' Doopin'
Harp: George Smith

Phone Blues	E
Blues in the Dark	A flat
Blues Away	E
Rockin'	E
California Blues	C
Oopin' Doopin'	G
Suzie Cross	D flat
Love Me	E
Down in N.O.	A flat
Found	D
Love	F
Ball	D

Bruce Springsteen
Darkness on the Edge of Town
Harp: Bruce Springsteen

Badlands	A
Adam	A
Something	C
Candy	F
Racing	B flat
Promised Land	C
Factory	F
Streets	D
Prove It	D
Darkness	C

Bruce Springsteen
Greetings from Asbury Park
Harp: Bruce Springsteen

Blinded	A
Growing Up	F
Arkansas	G
Bus Stop	C
Flood	C
Angel	C
For You	B flat
Spirit	A
Saint	D

Southside Johnny & the Asbury Jukes
This Time It's for Real

This Time	C
Without Love	B flat
Popeye	F
First Night	F
She's Got	D
Some Things	A
Little Girl	A
Fever	D
Love	C
Dance	C

Cross Harp

Bill Tarsha Rocket 88's
Let's Rumble
Harp: Bill Tarsha

Cookin'	D
Rumble	A
You Don't	G*
Walk In	E flat
Don't Know	B flat
Tongue	A
Breakout	D
Love	F
Elmo	A
Road	G*
That's All	E

We believe Bill plays a "C" chromatic in key of D. Listing is for regular cross harp.

Sonny Terry
Blind Sonny Terry
Harp: Sonny Terry

Cornbread	A
Ham	A
Lost John	A
Chain Gang Blues	A
It Takes a Chain	A
Betty Dupree	A
Stickhole	A
Rock Me	A
Chain Gang Special	G
Long John	A
Pick a Bale	A
Red River	A

Sonny Terry
Whoopin'
Harp: Sonny Terry

Eyes	B
Whoopin'	A
Burnt	C
Whoee	C
Crow	B
Tough	B
Whoee	C
Got Blues	A
Ya Ya	A
Roll Baby	B

Muddy Waters
Hard Again
Harp: James Cotton

Mannish Boy	D
Bus Driver	A
Wanna Be Loved	F*
Jealous	D
Satisfied	D
Blues Baby	D
Florida	C
Cross Cut	C
Little Girl	D

The listing is for Cross Harp, but James plays a "C" chromatic in the key of C on this number.

Muddy Waters
The Best of Muddy Waters
Harp: Little Walter

Just Make Love	G*
Long Distance	B flat
Louisiana Blues	D
Honey Bee	B flat
Rolling Stone	A
I'm Ready	A flat**
Hoochie Coochie	D
She Moves Me	B flat
I Want You	C
Standing	B flat
Still a Fool	B flat
Can't Be Satisfied	C

Little Walter plays chromatic Third Position. on the diatonic, play your G harp Cross Harp.
**Walter played C chromatic in pressed position D flat. Play Cross Harp diatonic on your A flat harp.*

Sonny Boy Williamson
Bummer Road
Harp: Rice Miller aka Sonny Boy Williamson II

Next to Me	B flat
Santa Claus	D
Little Village	F
Lonesome Road	F
Can't Do	D
Temperature	F
Unseen Eye	C
Hand Out	B flat
Open Road	E
This Old Life	E

Sonny Boy Williamson and the Yardbirds
Harp: Rice Miller aka Sonny Boy Williamson II

Bye Bye	C
Cool Blue	F
Stop	F
Eyesight	F
Memphis	D
Cross Heart	F
Crazy	C
9 below	F
Long Time	C
The Dead	F
Stop Baby	C
Down Child	C
Pontiac	F
Close	C

Neil Young
Hawks and Doves
Harp: Neil Young

Little Wing	E flat
Homestead	G
In Space	F
Kennedy	B flat
Staying	C
Coastline	F
Man	C
Coming	C
Jawks	C

Resources for Harp Players

www.gindick.com
An ongoing learning, listening and shopping center for students of the harmonica, and the best way to have contact with Jon as you learn.

www.harmonicalessons.com
An excellent resource for anyone learning to play.

The World Wide Web
Simply search on the word "harmonica" to find a plethora of real things, pretenders and those in between.

Masterclass Workshop www.harmonicamasterclass.com
Summer workshop lets you meet with some of the best players in the world. 877-427-7552.

SPAH, Society for the Preservation of the Harmonica
PO 865 Troy, MI 48099 www.members.aol.com/harmonica/
SPAH is an instant and inexpensive membership into the harp community, with a great summer bash and regional harp clubs.

Online Chatrooms on harp. Find out just how crazy the harp world is.
Harp-L: send e-mail to majordomo@garply.com with message "subscribe harp-l"
Harp-Talk: www.egroups.com/group/harptalk/

Online Retailers
Kevin's Harps: www. Kharps.com 1-800-274-2776
Harp Depot: www.harpdepot.com 1-800-783-7996

Send for catalogs:
Hohner Harmonicas PO 15035, Richmond, VA 23227
Lee Oskar Harmonicas PO 50225, Bellevue, WA 98015
425-747-6867/425-747-7059

For advanced studies, I recommend teachers Joe Filisko, Howard Levy, David Barrett, Glenn Weiser and many others. See your local music store for harps, teachers, vintage tube amps and other harp equipment.

Rock n' Blues Harmonica Volume II

"Rock n' the Folk," an Amplified Harp/Band CD Lesson with 24-page CD Booklet. $15.95

This CD experience takes you to an advanced level in a spectacularly easy way. The goal is to learn to play and improvise on melodies played blues and jazz style.

With Jon in charge, you learn the cross harp way to play songs like "Red River Valley" and "Home on the Range." Holding the master's hand, you walk patiently through each single note and bend. Then you begin to integrate blues riffs into the melody, using bends, unbends, head-shakes, octaves, octave head-shakes, articulation and chording to turn the song into blues harp. Finally, you try it all out jamming to blues and jazz jam tracks with drums, bass, piano and guitar.

The illustrated CD booklet might be small but it is good! It explains basic music theory and harmony in ways everyone can understand, and it shows several ways to play each song. It is richly illustrated and provides notation of every song and riff plus improvisational options and guitar chords. A winner for everyone who can play a single note.

Rock n' Blues Harmonica Volume III

"Jon's Jam Room" Lessons, Jam-along and Jam Tracks CD and 16-page CD booklet. $15.95

On this 73-minute CD lesson, Jon's band, Cross Harp Conspiracy, plays six backing tracks in major and minor keys, and each track is presented three times.

The first time, Jon gives you a lesson over the track, showing you basic riffs and then getting more advanced. The second time, Jon jams with the track. The third time, there is no harmonica, just you and the music. You be wailing! Each backing track is good, rich music, fun and easy to jam with. You'll learn new riffs, learn to jam with different kinds of musical styles and develop confidence and ability with every playing.

The CD booklet is an extraordinarily useful little thing. The meticulous indexing gives you lots of ways to study the lessons and transfer your knowledge into the jams, plus each riff is notated.

More Jamming for Harp Players

60-Minute Cassette Lessons With Information Sheets

Harp and Guitar Jam Volume I Jam with Jon to seven different guitar chord progressions. Includes country, jazz, rock, folk and blues styles. For C and G harps. 60 minutes...$9.50

Harp and Guitar Jam Volume II–Exclusively Cross Harp Features blues, boogie, rock jams and tips on bending, tongue-blocking and riff making. Easy guitar music to jam with. For A harp...$9.50

Four Positions of Blues, Rock and Jazz Harp Take a step into more advanced harmonica by learning to play songs and riffs in 1st, 2nd, 3rd and 5th positions. Includes easy guitar music to jam with. For C harp...$9.50

The Robert Johnson Lesson Teaches seven Robert Johnson Blues Classics. Includes "Rollin' and a Tumblin'," "Sweet Home Chicago," "Love in Vain," "Come into My Kitchen" and more. Includes easy guitar music to jam with. For C harp...$9.50

Gospel Plow This two-volume set teaches the Cross Harp way to play gospel standards "Kum Ba Yah," "Just a Closer Walk," "What a Friend We Have in Jesus," and many others. Includes easy guitar music to jam with. $14.95 for two tapes.

Get the set for $39.95, or each lesson at listed price. Information sheets include notation, lyrics and essential lesson information.

Blues Harp, The Movie

60-Minute VHS video
BB King and Jon Gindick

Blues guitar legend BB King teamed with Jon and made this superb instructional video to let you see and hear detailed instruction on the basics of the blues harp. This program, covering single notes, bending and basic riffs, has provided the breakthrough for many beginners.

For C harp...$24.95

Harmonica Americana

LEARN TO PLAY AMERICA'S 30 GREATEST SONGS

by Jon Gindick
176 page book, 2 CDs (or tapes)
40 minute video

Do you need something a tad easier? Pull up a chair 'cause "Doc" Gindick is going to teach you to **beautifully** play the American classics. It's a 176 page **book and double CD kit** created by the fictional "Doc" who travels the **Old West** selling harmonicas at a nickel each and teaching folks to play 'em. The book includes illustrated instruction ontechniques, song notation, lyrics, guitar chords, history of harmonica, easy-play harp notation–plus a section on blues and train music.

The two richly mastered CDs are each more than an hour long. Volume I gives you a **slow and easy lesson** on the techniques and walks you very slowly through each song. Volume II plays each song on **guitar, voice and harp** for your play-along and listening pleasure.

The **40 minute video** lets you see the techniques–single notes, bending, moving the harmonica–and provides some great jams on these famous tunes.

Book with 2 CDs $24.95 Add Video $15.00

The songs you'll learn and play:
America
Star Spangled Banner
Auld Lang Syne
Down in the Valley
Yankee Doodle
Home on the Range
Shenandoah
Danny Boy
Beautiful Dreamer
Old Grey Mare
Oh Susanna
Battle Hymn of
   the Republic
Turkey in the Straw
When Irish Eyes
   Are Smiling
On Top of Old Smokey
Down in the Valley
Frankie and Johnnie
Dixie
Old Folks at Home
Camptown Races
Bill Bailey
Brahms Lullaby
and many more.

Send check, money order or credit card information to:

Cross Harp Press, 530 Ranch Road, Visalia, CA 93291

$6.95 shipping on all orders.
Call 800-646-9245 or fax 818-886-0085
For updated information, visit our website at www.gindick.com
Email jfgindic@ix.netcom.com

Major Key Diatonic Note Location

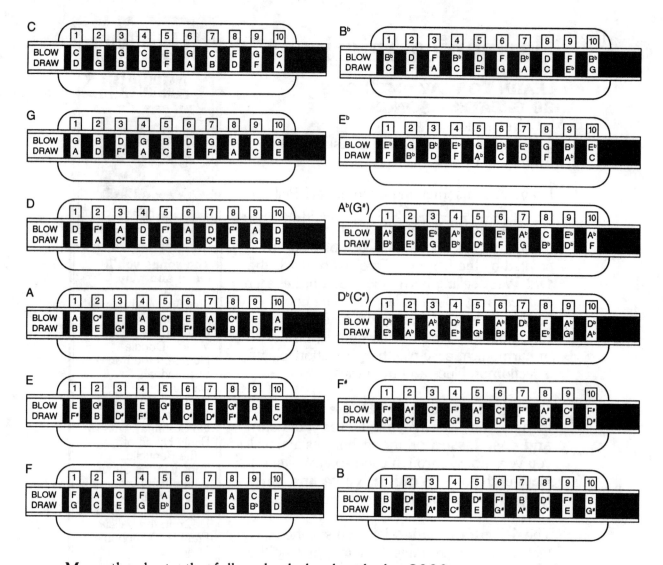

Many thanks to the folks who helped with the 2000 revision including, but not limited to, Karen Gindick, my wife, editor and friend, John Starkweather of Advanced Design Concepts, Boris Menart, who mixed and mastered the CD, and the many harp players and students whose playing, advice, encouragement, musical passion and feedback has inspired the information on many of the pages in this book. The online harmonica talk service, Harp-L, brought to me the wisdom and experience of many of our finest players. Blues Harmonica has a great tradition extending back beyond the turn of the century. At the root of this tradition are the harp players, guitar players and singers who, out of the most difficult human circumstances, forged the music that has grown into modern blues, jazz and rock and roll.

Index of 2nd Position Riffs

The purpose of this list is to help you practice solo and with the CD. In the real world, these riffs are jumping off places for riffs of your own. They change depending on how they are being used.

I chord 1234d   **IV chord** 1234b   **V chord** 456d

Beginner's Blues Riff 3b 4d 2d

Up Riff 3b 3d 4b 4d   **Down Riff** 4d 4b 3d* 3b

Incomplete Down 4d 4b 3d (play 3x, third time, resolve on 3b or 2d)

4 Draw Surprise 4d 4b 3d 4d   **Surprise Resolution** 4d 4b 3d 6b

6 Blow Down 6b 5d 4d 4b 3d 3b   **6 Blow Wailer** 6b 5d 4d

5 Draw Mistake 2d 3d 4b 4d 5d 4d   **Good Morning Riff** 1d 2b 2d

Good Morning 3d 1d 2b 2d 3d   **Good Morning 4d** 1d 2b 3d 4b 4d

9 Blow Down 9b 9d 8b 8d 7d 6d 6b   **6 Blow Up** 6b 7d 8d 8b 9b

Blues Scale Down 9b 9d 8b 8d 7d 6d 6b 5d 4d 3d 2d 1d 2b 3d 2d

Blues Scale Up 1d 2b 2d 3d 4b 4d 5d 6b 7d 8d 8b 9b

7ths Based Up and Down 2d** 2d 3d*   3d 2d 2d**

Rockin' Robin Riff 5d 5b 4d 5b 5d 5b 4d

Bent 6 Draw Down 6d* 6d 6b 5d 4d 4b 3d* 2d

Bent Up Riff 2d** 2d 3d* 4b 4d* 4d

Bent Down Riff 4d* 4d 4b 3d* 2d 2d**

Bent Wailing Riff 4d* 4d 5d 4d 5d 4d* 4d

Little Walter Riff 2d 3d 2d 2d** 2d 3d** 2d

Super VII Riff 3d* 2d 2d** 2d 3d* 2d 2d**

9 Blow Surprise 4d 4b 3d* 9b

Tongue Blocks 3-6b 1-4d 2-5d 6-9b

---

b means blow
d means draw
* means bend 1 step
** means bend 1½ steps

Substitute 2d for 3b as you improve.

Stereo CD/Book Index

Section I Slow Jam
The band (bass, drums and guitar) is in the key of G7. Play 2nd position, C harp.

1. Acoustic Jam
2. Electric Jam
3. Ground Rules
4. Type Harmonica (35)
5. Acoustic harp explanation (132, 133, 190)
6. Amped harp (190, 134)
7. **Word to beginners**
8. Band's I-IV-V progression (27)
9. Cross Harp Draw Chord (42)
10. Tone Techniques (38)
11. I-IV-V Harp Chords (42)
12. V chord, IV chord (42)
13. Draw Blow Draw breath patterns
14. Connecting Harp to Body (47)
15. Embouchures (47-50)
16. Single Note 4 draw (47)
17. Compressed air column (49)
18. Vibrato (49)
19. Articulation (49)
20. Attack and Decay
21. 3 blow single note
22. Soft Loud Soft Cry
23. **First day's lesson ends**
24. 3 draw single note
25. 2 draw single note
26. 5 draw, 4 draw slide
27. Moving harmonica
28. 6 blow, 3 blow, 9 blow
29. 2 draw to 3 draw
30. Swing Low, Sweet Chariot (57)
31. Pentatonic Scale (57)
32. Beginner's Blues Riff (76)
33. Up Riff, Down Riff (76,79)
34. Don't Accent 4 blow
35. 4 and 5 draw riffs (81)
36. Headshake (196)
37. 4 draw Surprise (83)
38. Good Morning Riffs (84)
39. 6 blow Riffs (87-90)
40. 9 blow Riffs (92-99)
41. Swing Low with riffs
42. Bending (116-119)
43. 4 draw bending (119-120)
44. 3 draw bending (121-123)
45. 2 draw bending (124-125)
46. Some Riffs on page 130
47. 6 draw Bend Down (127)
48. 9 blow Down (128)
49. Stop and Start scales (130)
50. Hand Effects (132-134)
51. Tongue Block Single Note (50, 194)
52. Tongueslap (194)
53. Octaves 3-6b, 1-4d, 2-5b (195)
54. T-B vs. Pucker
55. Band with no harp

Section II
56. **Fast Jam Shuffle and easier riffs**
57. Broom Duster Riff (130)
58. Shortnin' Bread (163)
59. Frankie and Johnnie (165)
60. 5d Rockin' Riff (126)
61. Broom Duster (130)

Section III
62. **Minor Key Jam (Music in G minor)**
63. Second position 3d bend
64. Easier Riffs
65. Red River Valley Vocal
66. Tongue-blocking
67. Minor key play-along
68. Conclusion

> To hear band only, adjust stereo balance to right. To hear harp and instruction only, adjust to left. Listening and playing along all three ways should be a big help in your learning. Good luck!